Things Unshakable

Things Unshakable

and Other Sermons

by

PAUL STROMBERG REES, D. D.

Author of *If God Be For Us!*, **etc.**

WM. B. EERDMANS PUBLISHING COMPANY
Grand Rapids   **Michigan**

THINGS UNSHAKABLE
by PAUL STROMBERG REES, D.D.

Acknowledgments

For permission to quote their copyrighted works, the author wishes to express his appreciation to the following publishers:

To Abingdon-Cokesbury Press for quotations from *This Is the Victory* by Leslie D. Weatherhead and *Abundant Living* by E. Stanley Jones.

To Charles Scribner's Sons for the poem *Our Daily Bread* by Maltbie D. Babcock.

To Dodd, Mead & Company for a quotation from *The Woman and the Angel* by Robert Service.

To Harper & Brothers for a quotation from *When the Morning Wakens* by Malcolm James MacLeod.

To Fleming H. Revell Company for quotations from *God's Control* by Samuel Shoemaker.

Any failure to give proper credit is due either to inadvertence or to my inability to trace the source.

CONTENTS

FOREWORD

During the war a map-publishing company sold its atlas under the catchy slogan: "The Book Behind the Headlines." Actually, of course, the one Book that is behind all the events of history's passing parade is the Bible.

It is from this Book, as being preeminently and perennially the preacher's "source book," that the following sermons derive both text and texture. They were preached, from time to time, on Sunday mornings during, and just following, the war. They are bound together by no unity other than that of their central loyalty to the eternal gospel of Jesus Christ our Lord. They aim to throw up, against the background of the world's shifting — and often shattering — headlines, the unshakable verities of our Christian message.

Those who first heard these addresses were the members of the congregation of First Covenant Church, in Minneapolis. together with an uncounted audience which forms the radio circle of a church that has been broadcasting its Sunday morning services for the past six years.

Appreciation cannot here be expressed by name to my friends who have so earnestly urged the publication of another volume of radio sermons. I must not fail, however, to acknowledge gratefully the valuable assistance of my secretary, Miss Mercedes Fouks, and the generous congregation which makes her services possible.

PAUL S. REES

PASTOR'S STUDY, FIRST COVENANT CHURCH,
MINNEAPOLIS, MINNESOTA.

I.

"Things Which Cannot Be Shaken"

Text: *"And this word, Yet once more, signifieth the removing of those things that are shaken . . . that those things which cannot be shaken may remain.*—HEBREWS 12:27.

IT IS no small victory that a man wins if he can stand amid the ruins of a dream, or a home, or a business, or a civilization, and say, "Even so, I have my hand on something that remains." Early in the late war we heard a good deal about the Norwegian seaport of Narvik. It was seized by the Germans, bombarded by the British, bombed again and again by planes. One day the mayor of the city, surrounded by newspaper men, stood in the midst of the wreckage. Glancing first at the desolation that lay about him and then at the snow-clad peaks that looked serenely down from the heights, he uttered these simple words: "The mountains are still ours."

That is the wisdom of a great soul. It is the discerning faith that sees beyond the fleeting shadow to the abiding substance, beyond things shaken to the things that are unshakable.

Such faith and such discernment were in the soul of the Christian thinker who gave us our text. The author of the letter to the Hebrews had lived in a religious world that was being shaken to its foundations. He was writing as a Hebrew to Hebrews. Together they had become Christians. As Christians they were faced with the claim that Jesus Christ was greater than Moses, that the covenant of grace was superior to the covenant of the law, that the offering of Christ upon the Cross was more precious than the offering of the blood of bulls and goats. They were faced with the claim that Moses and his ritual of animal sacrifices had a certain typical and temporary meaning, but that Jesus and His revelation of the redeeming grace of God had a consummating and eternal value.

You Christians, cries this flaming-hearted apostle, must realize that the living God has stretched out His hand to shake the old order of things and, out of the shaking, to bring in something unutterably precious and permanent. You have not come — you who have taken Jesus Christ as your Mediator and Saviour — to Mount Sinai, "the mount that might be touched." You are come to "Mount Sion," to the "heavenly Jerusalem." You are not come to Moses. You are come to "Jesus the mediator of the new covenant, and to the blood of sprinkling, that speaketh better things than that of Abel." It is a time of shaking! You cannot escape it. Here it is. You must come to terms with it.

As if this were not enough, the author of our text was about to witness the violent overthrow of that beloved city of Jerusalem which symbolized the long tradition and the solemn glory of his ancestral faith. The legions of a pagan power — Rome — were getting ready to lay the city in ruins, to kill its inhabitants by the thousands and to scatter to the four winds those whom they did not destroy. He saw that such terrific upheavals would raise questions in many a mind. Has all of this violence and disruption any meaning? If it has, does it mean that *everything* is falling apart, that nothing is dependable, that God Himself has abdicated, or else has never existed, except perhaps in our poor deluded minds?

No, cries this steadfast apostle of the first century, it signifies nothing of the kind. God is alive! God is about! God is not idle! God is fulfilling His Word! Not everything that is happening is what He would like to have happen. But

12

nothing that is happening is wholly removed from His will. In this sense the shaking is *His*. And it has its purpose. He is shaking the things that can be moved in order to uncover the things that can never be shaken.

Now you and I greatly need this Christian conviction and insight as we stand today "amid the encircling gloom" of this desperately troubled and tumultuous day. A question of utmost importance to every one of us is this: How are we reacting to the tremendous shakings which these days are visiting upon us? Or, to change the question, how *should* we respond to them and how *will* we respond to them if we have within us the seed of a genuine Christian faith?

I.

Suppose we start with this: We need the sheer *grit* to face the facts with respect to the shakings that are taking place.

Glance around at the social and economic world, and you get the impression that an earthquake has struck. Millions of our girls and women removed from home and school to factory and mill! Easy money, easy liquor, and easy morals combining to send our divorce court statistics to all-time heights! A sharp switch from a depression economy in which we had breadlines and WPA's to a war-created prosperity in which we have factory girls in fur coats and bellhops getting manicures! A sudden abandonment of the gold standard and a spending spree in which the national debt soars to an approaching three hundred billion dollars! An attack upon Pearl Harbor, and a hundred and twenty-five million people find themselves unable to buy automobiles, or tires for the ones they have already! Thousands of business places closed, their operators either taken in the draft or forced to the wall by wartime restrictions and shortages! The whole economy of business and trade regimented, restricted, and controlled under the war emergency powers exercised by the federal government. And now the confusions, tensions and turmoils of "reconversion." All of this produces an impact which hits more or less violently at every home in the nation and at every individual within that home.

Or look at the international scene. The concussion of the block-busters dropped by B-29's and the ghastly devastation of the atomic bomb might be taken as a symbol and a measure of the upheaval and suspense which the war has brought to the nations on all continents. Wholly aside from the frightful ravages of the war itself, there are the countless complications which are the invariable by-products of war. We have had governments in exile and revolutionists in power. We have had puppet governments and Quisling regimes in countries where the dictators have had control, and we have division and confusion in the so-called liberated lands where the Allies have the upper hand. We have, now that the fighting is over, an increasingly determined scramble for power and profits. All of which gives point and substance to the recent remarks of a social research expert who declared, "The war will have solved no basic problems. As a matter of fact, it will have made a good many of them more complicated. . . . To expect otherwise is like expecting that pneumonia will have cured the physical debility that brought it on."

Or turn for a moment to the realm of religion. Through the early part of this century theological liberalism held sway. It had a philosophy, a theology, and a psychology that were all sugar and no salt. It had a sugary philosophy of history: history was a march of inevitable progress. It had a sugary theology about God: God was a being of such melting tenderness that there could be no hell in His universe and, no matter what men might do, He would somehow see them through to a very happy end. It had, moreover, a sugary psychology of man: man was, after all, not a really sinful being who needed to be changed in a spiritual rebirth, but a being essentially good who needed only to have that good brought out by education and by improvements in his environment.

But two world wars in one generation have shaken "the very daylights" out of that easy-going and un-Biblical liberalism. Listen, for example, to the testimony of a converted liberal whose delicate painted-glass theology was smashed to pieces by the ghastly events connected with the present war: "I know beyond any possibility of doubt that Humanism is a false faith and that Christian Liberalism is an aberration and an abortion. Not all the king's horses nor all the king's men can put that particular humpty-dumpty together again. For me, Humanism and modernism were shattered beyond hope of repair. I have submitted evidence which I claim puts beyond doubt the fact that human nature has evil in its fibre and structure."

That is what I mean by having the grit to face the facts when God's shakings are loose in the world. Dr. Davies faced them and, with a brave honesty, did something about them. He has given the world a forthright confession of his conversion to Bible-centered faith.

What will *you* do with the facts as they close in upon your life? Some of us are so afraid of changes that we always run from them. We take the foolish position that the old way, whatever it is, is always good enough. This swift-paced era is dreadfully hard on such persons. It is breaking them down, so that all they do is sulk or scold.

Some of us, on the other hand, try to make the best of changes that are forced upon us, but we do so with the thought that when the crisis is past, we will promptly return to the "good old days." That, too, may be a very stupid and disappointing course to follow. Yet it is the course being followed right now by some of our die-hard business men and by some of our Tory-minded statesmen. I am far from suggesting that all of the changes that are emerging from the war are for the good, but I feel I am doing my friends a service if I say to them emphatically that it is a vain thing to dream of going back to the same old U.S.A. or the same old world that we had before Munich and Pearl Harbor.

Out of these shakings, we may be sure, will come a changed order of things. If *man* has his way in setting up the new order, it will last for a while and then it, too, will be jolted into collapse. If God has *His* way, on the other hand, then we shall see that love has greater survival value than hate, that justice is more enduring than cunning and craftiness, that decency outlives indecency, and that cooperative good will yields more permanent dividends that ruthless competition. We shall see, to use the language of St. John, that "the fashion of this world passeth away," but "he that doeth the will of God abideth forever."

II.

Digging into our text a bit further, we discover another requirement if we are to stand up when times of shaking are upon us. We need not only the grit that faces the facts but also the *grip* that holds to the things that are unshaken and unshakable. The disappearance or destruction of some things, says our writer, should serve to throw into bolder relief the things that are indestructible. "That the things which cannot be shaken may remain!" What are they?

1. For one thing, in God's Son Jesus, we have *an unshakable Person*. With what thrilling confidence the apostle cries, "But ye are come to Jesus!" The figure of Moses fades out, but the figure of Jesus is destined to loom larger and larger for ever and ever. A score of years ago Dr. W. E. Orchard of England declared, "Christ may exhaust this world: this world will never exhaust Christ." He was right.

Other leaders live and die; Jesus died and lives eternally, adequate in His power to make our lives what they ought to be and faithful to us unto the end. Some Philadelphia newsboys, waiting in a little shack for their bundles in the early morning, made it a practice to tune in on George Palmer's gospel broadcast. They grew fond of the theme song, "Jesus Never Fails." One of them, a Jewish lad, became particularly attached to the broadcast and to the message of that simple song. When Mr. Palmer began giving out plaques on which were inscribed the words, "Jesus Never Fails," they sent for one and put it up over the radio.

Then one day Palmer received a letter from the group, telling him that this little fellow had just died and that they had taken care that the plaque was placed by the side of his body in the casket. In their unsophisticated way of talking, they said that they wanted their preacher to know that they had sent one of his plaques "up to heaven"! What they were really saying was that their little pal, having taken Christ as his Saviour, had proved in life and in death the truth of the theme song — "Jesus Never Fails." Unshakable is the person of Christ.

2. Consider further that in God's love we have *an unshakable peace*. Reaching back into the larger context of this chapter, we come upon this gem: "For whom the Lord loveth he chasteneth, and scourgeth every son whom he receiveth" (v. 6). The Christian does not claim that he immediately understands the whole meaning of his suffering: he only claims that, since he is in God's hands, the suffering does have a meaning. Somehow God is right in there with him in his trouble, loving him, strengthening him, adding stature to his character and understanding to his soul.

"In this world," said Bacon, "God only and the angels may be spectators." Bacon was wrong. The God I see in the drawn and pain-filled face of that glorious Man upon the Cross is no mere spectator gazing from afar upon the ills and distresses of His children. Not *spectator* but *participator* is this Father-God of ours! In the confidence of His unfail-

17

ing love I can carry on, whispering the while, "Yea, though I walk through the valley of the shadow of death, I will fear no evil: for thou art with me." It is enough — this Love that will not let me go!

3. And then something else belongs among the unshaken things: in God's holiness we have *an unshakable principle*. "Follow peace with all men," says verse 14, "and holiness, without which no man shall see the Lord."

Our Canadian poet, Robert Service, has drawn a vivid picture of a masculine angel who, growing tired of golden harps, crowns and streets, came down to wander among earth's human creatures. Service pictures that angel falling into the toils of a thoroughly "liberated" modern girl. She tempts him, but in the midst of it the angel suddenly draws back, saying, "This is wrong, and I know it is wrong." Then the poet gives us her cynical response:

> *"Then sweetly she mocked his scruples, and softly she him beguiled:*
> *'You, who are verily man among men, speak with the tongue of a child.*
> *We have outlived the old standards; we have burst, like an over-tight thong,*
> *The ancient, outworn, Puritanic traditions of Right and Wrong.'"*

"We have outlived the old standards," so we say. But have we? Not by as much as one split second! To be sure, we have scorned them. We have done our best to scuttle them. "Holiness," we have scoffed, "how stupid and old-fashioned that sounds — and how unsufferably dull! It isn't holiness that we want; it's happiness. Happiness wherever we can find it: if we can't find it on Decency Drive or Sobriety Street, we'll go to Rotten Row!"

But all the while holiness of heart and life remains, like some calmly splendid star, among the immovables of life. All the while there is something deep within us that keeps saying:

"I know that right is right,
That it is not good to lie;
That love is better than spite,
And a neighbor than a spy;

I know that passion needs
The leash of a sober mind;
I know that generous deeds
Some sure reward will find;

In the darkest night of the year,
When the stars have all gone out,
That courage is better than fear,
That faith is truer than doubt;

And fierce though the fiends may fight,
And long though the angels hide,
I know that Truth and Right
Have the universe on their side."

Yes, among the unshakables be sure to put down the principle of Christian holiness.

4. And then one more thing: in God's Word we have *an unshakable proclamation.* "See that ye refuse not him that speaketh," is the burning admonition of our writer in verse 25. He knows his history, does this dead-in-earnest apostle. He knows that God has always a "Word" for men in the day of their need. God had a "Word" for men at Mount Sinai, and He spoke it in the Law. God had a "Word" for men in the dark days of the Captivity, when His people were languishing in Babylon, and He spoke it, says our author, through the prophet Haggai. Just when Jerusalem was a shambles, and Solomon's Temple was in ruins, and the future of Israel seemed most hopeless, came the Word of the Lord like a trumpet, announcing that He would shake things into life and hope, and a grand new destiny would take shape among the ashes of their plight.

It was proclaimed with assurance that a new temple would rise upon the foundations of the old. It did. It was proclaimed that "the Desire of all nations" should come — the Lord Jesus Christ. And He came! "Don't you see it?" argues the apostle with his fellow Christians, "God has given us His Word — the Word of His Son, Jesus Christ — and we may rely upon it, live by it, yes, if need be, die by it." "Refuse not him that speaketh."

That message is for *us*, too. The time-tested wisdom of the Holy Scriptures is for *us*. The solemn warnings against folly and iniquity are for *us*. The "exceeding great and precious promises" are for *us*. This Book of God has never been outmoded or invalidated. It is, as Paul Scherer admirably suggests, not the "Book of the Month": it is the "Book of the Ages."

In the eighteenth century Voltaire wrote, "In one hundred years the Bible will be an extinct book." Well, if a man could be more ridiculously mistaken than that, it is hard to see how! Recently, at an auction in London, a 95-volume set of Voltaire's writing, bound in calfskin, sold for eight shillings. A little while before that, the British government had paid Russia more than $400,000.00 for the *Codex Sinaiticus*, an ancient manuscript of the Bible. History has a queer way of judging a man, doesn't it? And last year more than 25,000,000 copies of the Bible were sold. God shakes the things that are removable in order to reveal and confirm the things that cannot be shaken!

III.

As to the third major requirement for meeting successfully the days of shaking, it is named for us in these words which follow our text: "Wherefore we receiving a kingdom which cannot be moved, let us have grace, whereby we may serve God acceptably with reverence and godly fear." The *grit* to face the facts of our shaken world — we need that. The *grip* that clings to the things that cannot be shaken — we must have that. And then this very personal thing — the *grace* to be changed ourselves in conformity with the eternal pattern of God's heavenly kingdom.

"Let us have grace!" What for? Why, that we may "serve God acceptably." And this we cannot do unless we have been changed ourselves. Changed in that initial and decisive way in which conversion to Christ changes us? Yes! Changed in that still deeper way in which the sin-purging of the Holy Spirit, through the principle of the Cross, changes us? Yes! And then continuously changed in all of those countless ways in which our characters are tried and tested, sanded and polished, in the daily discipline of a consecrated life! And all this by drawing, in simple faith, upon the offered love and power of Jesus Christ our Lord! Only so can we hope to serve God acceptably.

A friend of mine was preaching in a certain city. More than 500 miles away was a lady who wanted to hear him and have an interview with him. Hers had been a shaken life for some time. She had been hit both by sorrow and sickness, and had gone down under the blow. Worry and fear had all but unbalanced her. In the conversation which took place at the end of a 550-mile drive, she unburdened her heart to the man of God in whom she had confidence. He saw that she was herself an unsurrendered, unchanged woman. Working with her quietly, through the Scriptures and through sympathetic counsel, he got her to yield herself to Christ. This was the testimony she later wrote to him:

"There has been no relapse since my coming home. This recovery is so real; it is not neurotic, for my nerves are becoming steady, and my heart is beginning to act like a normal heart should. It is wonderful. . . . When the doctor saw me yesterday, he said, 'Something has happened to you since you were here before. There is a transformation in you which is almost unbelievable. What is it?' When I told him, he said, 'I know what you say is true, for you yourself are the proof of it.' And then he added, 'What you have found is what seventy-five per cent of our patients need, for a great many of them would get well physically if they were well mentally and spiritually.' "

She was ready to meet — and master — life's hardest-hitting changes when, by the grace of God, she herself was changed.

"Let *us* have grace" that *we,* amid all the shocks of the present and the shakings of the future, may abide steadfast in the "things which are unshakable."

II.

The Angel in the Flame

~~~~~~

Text: *"And the angel of the Lord appeared unto him in a flame of fire out of the midst of a bush."*—EXODUS 3:2.

To SEE Moses at this period of his life is to see a man who has in him the making of greatness, but who needs to be touched with the flame of God's Spirit in order to set that greatness loose. He is without doubt a chosen vessel. Yet he is not, if we may borrow the language of the New Testament, a "vessel unto honor, sanctified, and meet for the Master's use, and prepared unto every good work."

The first period of Moses' life has long since passed and the second is nearing its end. In that first period it has been demonstrated that he is a child of Providence. By the law of Egypt he should have died; by the overruling of God he lived. Born a slave, he grew up a prince. The child of Hebrew parents, he was adopted into the royal family of Egypt.

Then, when offered a brilliant career as an Egyptian statesman, he deliberately chose the lonely and difficult lot of a defender of the Hebrew people. They were *his* people. They were slaves and not freemen. They needed a leader, a champion, an emancipator. Moses would espouse their cause and plead their case. But the high decision was almost immediately balked. Moses tried to do the job with man's weapons, not with God's. He tried anger and fists. They only got him into trouble. Finally, disgusted, frustrated, and full of fear, he fled to another country. There he settled down. There he took it easy. And yet *there* God overtook him.

He was forty years old when he left Egypt. Forty more years have passed over him out here in the desert. Still he is not prepared for the task God has for him. But a new crisis is at hand. It is the experience of which our text speaks. Let us look at it.

Here is Moses, a picture of many of us who are supposed to be in the Lord's service. It is a picture of enlistment in the cause of God which has nevertheless failed to bear fruit. It is a picture of good intentions defeated by wrong methods. It is a picture of too great reliance upon the energy of the flesh for doing what only the power of God can bring to pass. It is a picture of failure, discouragement, and complacency.

Then came the sudden change. The bush caught fire. Out of the fire God spoke. Moses saw. Moses listened. Moses was transfigured. He at last found himself. He found himself by losing himself; and he lost himself in God.

In studying this transforming experience that came to the man Moses, there are, chiefly, two considerations that I shall urge. One is the revelation that is symbolized by the burning bush; the other is the response that Moses made to this revelation.

I.

Consider first the character of the revelation which came to Moses through the medium of the flaming desert bush.

1. For one thing, that fire symbolized the revelation of a *Presence*. When Isaiah (63:8, 9) reviewed the history of Israel, he spoke of God as the "Saviour" of the children of Israel, and he adds, in beautiful phrase, "the angel of his presence saved them." This sense of the personal and intimate reality of God came to Moses with amazing power as he stood there before the flaming bush.

Never, after this encounter, could you persuade Moses that God is merely a noble concept, just a lovely ideal that we fashion out of wishful thinking. Never could you convince him that God is only a theory, an abstract theme about which philosophers may wrangle and theologians may dogmatize. Never could you make him believe that God, even if He does exist, is a far-away being who was needed to get the universe started but who actually is the great Untouchable, vastly beyond the reach of puny mortals like ourselves.

No, Moses was witness to the fact that God can communicate His presence to the soul of man as truly as any human friend that man ever had, and with far more meaning. If you wish, like Moses, to know His name, the answer comes, now as then, "I AM THAT I AM." He is the everlasting NOW and He is the everlasting YEA. As the everlasting NOW, He is above all death, all times and seasons, all "change and decay." He is the one who declares in the language of Christ, "I am Alpha and Omega, the beginning and the ending, saith the Lord, which is, and which was, and which is to come, the Almighty" (Revelation 1:8).

As the everlasting YEA, He affirms the final meaning of things: the universe, life, love, grace, judgment, and destiny. It was not given to Moses to receive the whole revelation. The affirmation was completed when, "in the fulness of time," God sent forth His Son. Then men heard again the mystic cadences of the great I AM, but now the music was more ample and simple. "I AM — the Way, the Truth and the Life." So it ran. "I AM — the bread of life." "I AM — the water of life." "I AM — the Good Shepherd." By these unveilings of truth God has reached the hearts of men. By them He has revealed the meaning and glory of all true living.

But let us get back to Moses. It is important that we see how utterly he must now depend upon the Presence as he goes forth from the burning bush. In verse 8 of the context he hears God saying to him, "*I* am come down to deliver (my people) out of the hand of the Egyptians." Ah, what a humbling insight that must have given to Moses! How swiftly his memory went back to the failure of forty years before. The trouble, as Moses now sees, was that *he* had gone out to deliver the people. There was too much of Moses about it — and too little of God.

Standing at that burning bush it all grows clear: Moses, as Moses, must die. He must die to himself, to his plans, to his methods, to his abilities. Out of that death will come a larger life — larger because its dimensions will not be those of self but those of God. Moses will not be in the picture at all except as the yielded instrument of God's purpose and power.

The question emerges: Have *we* come to our burning bush? Have *we* seen that in us dwelleth no good thing, but that Christ asks to take over the whole of our being and make it the holy dwelling-place of His own all-glorious and all-sufficient Presence? That question came to a man of God in Philadelphia years ago, and as a result his life and ministry were transfigured. It was none other than J. Wilbur Chapman, who at that time was pastor of Wanamaker Presbyterian Church. He knew that his dreams and desires for the ministry of God's Word in that church were not being fulfilled. Was the hindrance in himself? One day he fell to reading a sermon which Dr. F. B. Meyer had preached at the Northfield Bible Conference. Out of that printed sermon there leaped a sentence which, according to Dr. Chapman's own testimony, was to revolutionize his life and labors. It was this: "After all, it is not so much what we do for God that counts as it is what we let Him do through us." That sentence became to him what the burning bush was to Moses.

"I had been struggling for five years," says Chapman. "I had had visions of His power and glimpses of what I might be if I were 'filled with the Spirit,' but all this time, like the disciples at Ephesus, there was a great lacking. At last I reached the place where I felt that I was willing to make the surrender. I reached it by the path marked out by Mr. Meyer when he said, 'If you are not ready to surrender everything to God, are you ready to say, "I am willing to be made willing about everything"?' That seemed easy, and alone before God I simply said, 'I am willing.' Then He made the way easy. He brought before me my ambition, then my personal ease, then my home, then other things came to me, and I simply said, 'I will give them up.' And last of all, my 'will' was surrendered about everything. Then without any emotion . . . I said, 'My Father, I now claim from Thee the infilling of the Holy Ghost.' From that moment to this He has been a living reality."

Dr. Chapman then goes on to say that for him Bible study was new and preaching was new, for it all went on now in the sense of His indwelling Who had come to take possession of every yielded faculty and talent. The flame that spoke of the Presence had been kindled in his soul.

2. Again, the burning bush symbolized the revelation of a *Persistency*. "Behold, the bush burned with fire, and the bush was not consumed."

As Moses stood watching this amazing spectacle — what someone has called the "miracle of the unconsumed" — it was as though God were saying to him, "Moses, this flaming bush has a quality that you have lacked. It does not flicker out; it blazes on and on and on. Once you started out to do my work with a hot heart, but you ended up with a hot temper and disgust. Once you were possessed with the rapture of a splendid dream. The rapture cooled and the dream faded. But, Moses, if you will surrender fully to the fire of my love, if you will identify yourself with the patient, faithful purpose which I have for my people Israel, you will be the man that I can use."

Moses accepted the challenge. As a result we read in the gallery of heroes, the eleventh chapter of Hebrews, that he "endured, as seeing him that is invisible." He "endured"! In that powerful, penetrating, sanctifying experience of the glowing bush he had come upon the secret of an undiscourageable perseverance. He had found in God the power to see it through. His life and leadership had staying qualities which they sorely lacked in the days gone by.

Will you let this truth hit home to your heart? Is it true that you, like Moses, gave up when the going got rough and unexpected reverses were encountered? Your leadership was not accepted and followed as you thought it would be, so what did you do? Instead of examining your own soul, did you take the easy way out and begin to lay blame on others — with the result that today your life has no glow and no glory about it? We have church members all over this country who are moping in the corner when they ought to be out on the front lines fighting valiantly in the ranks of the Lord Jesus Christ. What a glorious day this would be for them, and for the needy folks they could serve, if they would let the Spirit of God rekindle the played-out fires, refurbish the faded dreams and revive the fallen hopes! They must somehow come to believe that Christ will send them marching into their tomorrows with a steadfastness of purpose which no force in earth or hell can turn aside. Then they can say:

> "Though giant rains put out the sun,
>   Here stand I for a sign.
> Though Earth be filled with waters dark,
>   My cup is filled with wine.
> Tell to the trembling priests that here
>   Under the deluge rod,
> One nameless, tattered broken man
>   Stood up and drank to God."

3. Still another thing that is symbolically revealed through the burning bush is the thought of *Possibility*. Was that humble acacia bush any different, before it burst into flame,

than a thousand other shrubs that might have been found on the heath? Probably not. It was the fire that made it notable. When it was kindled, it became the medium of God's holiness and power and will. Then, and only then, were its possibilities brought out.

Moses, by this time, was so far removed from his former self-sufficiency and brashness that he now pled his inferiority. He would excuse himself from God's call by pleading that he was unequal to the task. Specifically, he insisted that he was "slow of speech." God's eloquent reply was: "Look at the bush, Moses! Look at the bush! A little while ago it was just a plain old shrub to which nobody would have given a second glance. Now look at it. If I can do that with a bush, when once the bush is set aflame, I can take you, when once you are wholly in my hands, and I can make you a surprise to Pharaoh, a surprise to Israel, and a surprise to yourself."

To clinch the lesson, God gave Moses an additional demonstration. "What is that in thine hand?" said He. "Why, Lord, it is just my shepherd's rod." "Very well, cast it on the ground." Moses obeyed, and instantly his rod was a serpent. "Now, pick it up." If Moses were like most of us, he would not relish the suggestion. But he obeyed. Instantly it was his rod again. It was God's way of saying, "Dear fellow, if you will let me have you and manage you as you have managed that rod under my direction, I will take you and with you I will break the power of Egypt and humble the pride of Pharaoh."

And God did it — because Moses was willing. Moreover, God has been doing that sort of thing ever since. All He asks is a Gideon's band of three hundred and some broken pitchers: in the morning the Midianites will be in wild flight. All He asks is a shepherd's sling and some stones from the brook: before nightfall the profane Goliath will be a corpse. All He asks is that the widow's mite be willingly

given: the ages will never be allowed to forget her consecration. All He asks is a lad's lunch of a few barley cakes
and a small mess of fish: before sundown five thousand
hungry men will be fed and a surplus left over.

It takes *God* to bring out the possibilities! But, mark you,
even He cannot do it unless there is complete submission to
the control of His will and the touch of His hand. I make
bold to say that there are throngs of Christian people in our
churches who are living half-developed lives because they
have never fully let go of themselves and claimed from God
the baptism of fire that would kindle their whole being into
a leaping flame of dedicated living. The possibilities are
there, but they are dormant, unrealized, yes, even unsuspected.

My father, in his earlier ministry, had a very dear friend
who at forty years of age was plodding along as a storekeeper
in a quiet little town in eastern Ohio. He had been converted
in boyhood. He was a respected and active member of the
Quaker church in that community. His home, moreover,
was frequently opened for cottage prayer meetings. One evening, when such a service was being held, a visitor dropped
in. He told the group about a camp meeting he had recently
attended in New York State, where Christians were being
urged to make an entire consecration of themselves to God
and to claim by faith the infilling of the Holy Spirit for a
life of holiness and power.

Although the visitor was careful to explain that he had
not claimed or received any new blessing himself, his report
of what he had witnessed became a powerful challenge to
the merchant in whose home the people were gathered. It
drove that man to his Bible. It drove him to his knees.
It drove him to the confession of a deep lack in his own life.
God met him in an experience of the Holy Spirit similar to
that which came to J. Wilbur Chapman. The next Sunday
he met with his fellow-churchmen in the Quaker Meeting
House where it was customary to wait in silence for the

Spirit of God to move someone to speak. The merchant, "full of the Holy Ghost," was soon on his feet, bearing testimony to what had taken place in his life. He did it with such freedom and simple eloquence that the old Quakers marvelled. At the close of the meeting one of them was heard to say, "Why, David also is among the prophets!" Since his first name was David, the Scripture was all the more appropriate.

The result was that this layman, forty years of age, left his shop to become a preacher and an extraordinary winner of souls. During the next thirty years he was to travel over much of the nation in the ministry of Christ. He was to become an author of no mean ability and renown. He was to become singularly successful in leading young men and women into full-time service for God. By the time of his death it was known that more than one thousand ministers and missionaries had received their call under the teaching and influence of this fire-baptized man. At forty David Updegraff was a plodding storekeeper, whose possibilities in terms of preaching and teaching were not so much as dreamed of, either by himself or his friends. Then came his burning bush! What a magnificent release it gave to those latent talents which God was eager to employ!

Is it too much to believe that many another potential soul-winner, many another potential church leader, many another missionary, is hidden from our sight, waiting only for the touch of God's holy fire to kindle into incredible usefulness the possibilities that are there? Who will now follow Moses in his obedience to the vision that came to him?

II.

What was the *response* which Moses made to the revelation of the burning bush? It can be summed up briefly in three words: Attention, Action, Arrival!

First, there was *attention*. "He *looked*, and behold the bush burned with fire." The humdrum of his shepherd's life was suddenly broken by this spectacle. He gave it his attention long enough to be convinced that it was something worth following up. When he saw that it was not consumed, he was ready to take the next step. Are you as honest with yourself and with God as Moses was? Has God been trying to say something to you which you have not been willing to hear? The first step toward blessing is to get your eyes really open and keep them open.

Then comes *action*. Moses said, "I will now turn aside, and see this great sight." Attention is the forerunner of action. Moses *acted* in line with his light. That is important. Many of us act in the opposite way. The vision comes and we turn from it. No wonder that our light turns to darkness. To act in obedience and faith is the sure secret of getting somewhere with God.

Finally, there is *arrival*. When God saw that Moses meant business, that he was sincerely in quest of anything that was real, He spoke to him, saying, "Put off thy shoes from off thy feet, for the place whereon thou standest is holy ground." Moses had arrived at the place of holiness. It was God's holiness, to be sure; but it was henceforth to be a shared reality in Moses' life. Linked up with the God of holiness, Moses was to share the holiness of God. It is an amazing fact, but a *fact* nevertheless.

Oh, Church of God, let your eyes be opened to the burning bush which God kindles for you right in the wilderness of this world's spiritual deadness. What is Pentecost if it is not the Church's burning bush? What is the offer of the baptism of fire in and through the Holy Spirit if it is not your burning bush? Let this then be your prayer:

> "*O that in me the sacred fire*
> *Might now begin to glow,*
> *Burn up the dross of base desire*
> *And make the mountains flow!*

O that it now from heaven might fall,
  And all my sin consume!
Come, Holy Ghost, for Thee I call;
  Spirit of burning, come!

Refining fire, go through my heart;
  Illuminate my soul;
Scatter Thy life through every part,
  And sanctify the whole.

No longer then my heart shall mourn,
  While, purified by grace,
I only for His glory burn,
  And always see His face."

III.

Living in Three Worlds

11/10/89

Text: *"Paul, an apostle of Christ Jesus by the will of God, to the saints who are in Ephesus—faithful in Christ Jesus."*
—EPHESIANS 1:1 (Weymouth).

Our word "environment," which we get from the Latin through the French, means, quite simply and literally, "that which surrounds." It may be seen or unseen, but if it is an encompassing element of our experience it may be said to be part of our environment.

Let us imagine that you are a passenger on the *Queen Mary* crossing the Atlantic. Around you is the ship itself, which is carrying you to your destination. Around you also are your fellow passengers — kindly, let us suppose, companionable, helpful. Around you, too, is a third environment: the ocean, which at its very best, by its nature, requires a lot of power to get through, and which at its worst becomes a terrific threat to your ever reaching your desired harbor.

Now if you will take that crude illustration and set it down reflectively beside our text, you will have a kind of pattern of the threefold truth to be seen in these words of St. Paul's. The apostle says he is writing to those who are "in Christ Jesus." As Christians this is their first and, spiritually speaking, their closest environment. He says also that he is writing "to the saints." Here is the second environment: life lived in the fellowship of other Christians. But Paul further states that these believers, who are "in Christ" and

34

in fellowship with one another, are also "in Ephesus." This is their outermost environment. It is glaringly visible and capable of exerting a tremendous pressure.

Now go back to our simple parable. Christians are said to be *in* Christ — environed by His life, supported by His grace, guided by His Spirit — as the passengers on the *Queen Mary* are environed and upheld by the vessel for safe passage across the Atlantic.

Christians, moreover, are said to be *in* the society or communion of saints — that is, they are strengthened and inspired one by the other — much as the fellow passengers on the *Queen* find stimulus, enrichment, and good cheer in their pleasant comradeship.

And then Christians are said to be *in* "Ephesus" — surrounded by its evils, disciplined by its temptations, challenged by its paganism — just as the mighty *Queen* finds its progress resisted and its throbbing engines strained by the buffeting winds and waters that encompass it.

Here, then, is the Christian's "Triple Environment." I want to talk to you, as the Spirit of God may help me, about each of them in turn.

I.

Consider the first: *the Christian's life is lived "in Christ Jesus."*

Now, curiously enough, you can ask a man if he is *in* business, and he knows what you are talking about. You can ask him if he is *in* one of the professions, say, law or medicine, and he knows what you are talking about. You can ask him if he is *in* love, and if he is, he knows glowingly — I almost said drunkenly — well what you mean. *But,* if you ask the average man if he is *in* Christ, he is strangely mystified by your query. Perhaps I should say he is either embarrassed by his own lack of understanding or else he is ready to embarrass you by telling you roundly that you must be one of those religious "crack-pots." He may be a church member, too.

Yet, here is the interesting thing: the early Christians were perfectly at home with this phrase, "in Christ Jesus." Robert Menzies, in his book, *The Magnet of the Heart,* declares that in the epistles of Paul the expression "in Christ" occurs one hundred sixty-four times. A shining example is in the words, "If any man be *in Christ,* he is a new creation. Old things are passed away; behold they have become new."

The man who said that, and who got others to believe it, knew what he was talking about. Paul, in the days when he was Saul, was like a good many religious people that you and I know. He was both worried and wearied: worried as to whether he could struggle hard enough, keep commandments enough, do good works enough, to save his soul; and wearied because the whole thing seemed to be so futile and so disappointing. Like many another unhappy and insecure sectarian, he was trying to make up by persecution of the Christians for the fears and inadequacies he felt in his own heart.

Then the light dawned — that day on the Damascus Road. Suddenly there came to him the flaming insight that the way to a new start in life, with release from the plague of guilt and the impotence of self-effort, was through giving up to a Person. Decisively it broke upon him that the way to "be saved," if you will, was not that of struggle with precepts and prohibitions and programs and performances. It was the way, rather, of a personal meeting with a personal Christ issuing in a personal communion between him and Christ, in which he furnished the surrender and Christ furnished the strength.

To be sure, there were extraordinary and dramatic features connected with the sharp, shattering conversion that came to Saul of Tarsus. These outer details are never completely duplicated in any two conversions. Quite true it is also, that some childhood experiences of Christ occur so early that, in adult life one does not carry any vivid memory of the day or hour when one's shining moment arrived. It remains true, however, notwithstanding all the varieties of Christian experience, that no healthy, assured, and effective Christian life begins until we are somehow introduced to the Lord Jesus Christ Himself.

Dora Greenwell tells of a woman of eighty years who passed by faith into this new order of life in which one actually experiences the pardon, the peace, and the continuing presence of Christ. At eighty-four she attempted a stanza of poetry in which she makes this significant and pathetic confession:

> *"If you ask me how long I have lived in the world,*
> *I'm old, I'm very old.*
> *If you ask me how long I have truly lived,*
> *'Twill very soon be told;*
> *Past eighty years of age,*
> *Yet only four years old."*

Eighty years in the community where she resided, but only four years — "in Christ"!

Yet Christ, by His living presence through the Holy Spirit, wants to be the closest and most powerful environment that we can know. He wants us to be bathed in His love as the sunlight bathes and makes fragrant the flowers. He wants us to be rooted in His faithfulness as the vine is rooted in the rich, nourishing soil. He wants us to be invigorated by His inexhaustible life as the blood in our bodies is invigorated by the oxygen breathed in from the ever ample air about us.

And thus *we* may be said to be what those first-century Christians were to whom Paul was writing — "in Christ."

"In Christ" — for forgiveness!
"In Christ" — for peace!

"In Christ" — for holiness!
"In Christ" — for guidance!
"In Christ" — for service!
"In Christ" — for ever!

"The stars shine over the earth,
The stars shine over the sea,
The stars look up to the mighty God,
The stars look down on me;
The stars will live for a million years,
For a million years and a day,
But Christ and I shall live and love
When the stars have passed away."

He — the eternal Christ Himself — is our first and most intimate environment.

II.

Now take the second: *the Christian's life is lived in the fellowship of the saints.* "Paul, an apostle of Christ Jesus by the will of God, *to the saints* who are in Ephesus."

The other day in my reading I made what was to me a new discovery. My attention was called to the fact that this word "saint" is almost never used in the singular in the New Testament. The fact is all the more exciting when one remembers that one of the fanaticisms of the middle ages was the belief that a man or woman must go off into some self-imposed and lonely exile if he or she wanted to be a "saint." You see the original Christian church, as portrayed on the pages of the New Testament, knew no such action and practiced no such policy.

Of course, the early disciples had their seasons of privacy for the prayerful and meditative undergirding of their faith. That is not disputed. At the same time it is notably true that they made a great deal of the life in Christ which they shared in common. Together, in blessed, banded fellowship, they formed their communities of worship and benevolence.

They were socially minded in the best sense of that phrase. They formed the "church," the "ecclesia," meaning the "called out" ones, in Jerusalem, and the "church" in Antioch, and the "church" in Corinth, and the "church" in Ephesus, and so on.

Here, in these fellowships, whether in private dwelling or noble synagogue or in the open air, they sang together the simple hymns of their faith, prayed together the earnest prayers of their devotion, shared together the problems and responsibilities of their common lot, and went out together to win converts to Christ in the streets and bazaars of the city.

What about us today — we Christians who are supposed to be the spiritual sons and daughters of those disciples of long ago? We have better church buildings than they had. But how well do we attend our services? We have more and finer facilities for getting together than they had. But do we have as warm a friendliness and as eager a love? There are more of us numerically. But do we cultivate the solidarity and kindle the morale that they did?

No, we won't forget that they sometimes had their bickerings and their quarrelings, but the total impression they made was well expressed in the exclamation, "Behold, how they love one another!"

My fellow Christians, don't be indifferent to this second environment of the life of faith. We need each other. We were made for each other. We cannot thrive as sons of God without each other. "The truth is," said Dr. Clow of Edinburgh, "that the faith in Christ cannot be maintained without the fellowship of His people. The Christian life cannot survive without common prayer and common song. It thrives only by the ministry of the Word and the partnership in service." Those are strong words, but they have much to support them.

To all of this there is a corollary: whatever you do, do not cause or be the occasion of discord in this fellowship. Do not damage the brotherhood. For Christ's sake, and the sake of the world before whom we witness, be a healer and not a breeder of strife. George Whitefield and John Wesley had a theological disagreement. In the course of the controversy Wesley wrote Whitefield a strong letter. Now listen to this reply from Whitefield:

> *"My Honoured Friend and Brother:*
> *"For once hearken to a child, who is willing to wash your feet. I beseech you, by the mercies of God in Christ Jesus our Lord, if you would have my love confirmed towards you, write no more about the misrepresentations wherein we differ. . . . Will it not in the end destroy brotherly love, and insensibly take from us that cordial union and sweetness of soul, which I pray God may always subsist between us? How glad would be the enemies of the Lord to see us divided? Honoured sir, let us offer salvation freely to all by the blood of Jesus, and whatever light God has communicated to us, let us freely communicate to others."*

That, you see, is the spirit and message of a man who is becomingly sensitive to environment Number Two in the Christian way — the fellowship of the saints. It is the admirable passion of a loving soul who longs, with Paul, to "comprehend *with all saints* what is the breadth and length and depth and height, and to know the love of Christ which passeth knowledge."

III.

Think now of the third circle of our environment: *the Christian life must be lived in an unideal world.* Hence Paul writes in our text to the "faithful saints . . . in Christ Jesus" who are *"in Ephesus."* Even though some of the translations omit this phrase, and Weymouth puts it in parentheses, there is no one who disputes that the apostle was addressing Christians who dwelt in and around that ancient center of pagan culture and gilded sin.

"In Ephesus!" Here is the freezing and foaming water through which our *Queen Mary* must plow its way to the Harbor of Light. To be "in Christ" — this gives us our inextinguishable *light*. To be in the "communion of saints" — this gives us our immense *lift*. But to be "in Ephesus" — this gives us our inescapable *lot*.

We are never to imagine that being "in Christ" — saved, as we so often put it — means living in some ivory tower apart, where no chill winds of opposition will blow our way, where no enticements to evil will ever insinuate themselves. Nor are we ever to fancy that the fellowship of believers can be so constant and complete as to prevent the evil of the outer world from flaunting itself in our face or snapping at our heels as we walk its streets.

Ephesus was pagan. Ephesus was idolatrous. Ephesus was immoral. Ephesus was vulgarly prosperous. Mean tricks flourished in her market-places. Degrading sports were the shout and the thrill of her amusement haunts. Vile sensualities walked unabashed in her streets and were even winked at in her temples. Yet here, squarely in the murky middle of all this pagan godlessness, were these strong sons and daughters of Christian faith wearing the white flower of a blameless life. Their glory did not lie in the hope that they were going to be saints in heaven; it lay in the *fact* that they were "saints" — separated unto Christ — then and there, in Ephesus!

If there are weak, or wavering, or wondering Christians listening to this message, I have a reassuring word for you: take care of the first two environments, and this third one will never be able to beat you down. If you are in Christ and

in the supporting fellowship of helpful, enlightened, courageous Christians, the world can neither corrupt you nor
crush you. Upon the contrary, you will be able, by the
inworking energies of the Spirit of God, to offer a positive
witness of truth and righteousness in *your* Ephesus, wherever
that may be.

I share with you a narrative of thrilling beauty and power
which recently came to my desk from London. Florence Lee
Manners was a low-class actress in London's "East End."
Her father's name she never knew. Her mother had been
an actress, performing in the back-rooms of the "pubs" where
indecency was given a high rating. Florence, soon to be
billed as "Fairy Flo," became a dancer and a singer.

For a time her own conduct contrasted sharply with the
loose living of her mother, with whom she resided in two
tiny rooms. The mother, prematurely old, was drinking
heavily all the time. Then, one night, Florence came home
intoxicated. A quarrel followed. Next day the mother dis-
appeared. Three days later her drowned body was recovered
from the river.

Then began Florence's descent into the abyss. Her dissi-
pation knew no limits. She, too, like her mother, was the
entertainer of the rowdy back-room gang, until, with health
and physical attractiveness gone, even the old crowd no longer
gave her much of a hand.

Came an evening when, half-drunk, she was making her
hapless way down the street. Here, on the corner, was an
open-air service being conducted by some mission workers.
She stopped to listen. Fumbling in her pocket, Florence
produced a penny and handed it to one of the workers. The
worker chanced to be a woman of wealth and culture — an
ardent lover of Christ and a sensible lover of derelict humanity. With a grateful cheeriness she accepted the pittance, and
walked away with the drunken girl by her side. She took

her to a little chapel, stayed with her until she was sober, then told her, with quiet radiance, the good news of Christ and His Cross of love. Florence felt its power. She responded to its call. She surrendered the shattered bits of herself to the healing Saviour. She was — "born again."

Then came a strange test for the faith of those mission workers who had helped her to Christ. She insisted that there was an engagement she must keep. Where? At the "Tiger Music Room." They were aghast. That vile den! Still, she *would* go. There came the moment in the program when "Fairy Flo" was to do a dance. The men gave her some mild applause. One of them thrust a glass toward her. She waved it away. Turning to the man at the piano, she told him no accompaniment was needed. What was up? A queer hush came over the ill-smelling room. But no dancing did Florence do. No shady ballad came from her lips. Instead, with eager voice and lighted eye, she began to sing:

> *"There is a fountain filled with blood,*
> *Drawn from Immanuel's veins;*
> *And sinners, plunged beneath that flood,*
> *Lose all their guilty stains."*

The men were stunned. It gave her time to sing another stanza:

> *"The dying thief rejoiced to see*
> *That fountain in his day;*
> *And there may I, though vile as he,*
> *Wash all my sins away."*

Then riot broke loose. "She's mad!" cried some of the men. "Gone religious," sneered others. Drunken ones among them lurched forward to strike her. In a flash she was gone — never to reappear on the stage.

And here is the fine sequel. R. G. Burnett, who tells the story, reports that Florence lived for years in London's East End, not only victorious over every one of the old temptations, but bearing a triumphant and attractive testimony to the love of Christ which had redeemed her.

In Christ she found the *dawn* of life! In the fellowship of Christians she found the *development* of life! In Ephesus she found the *discipline* of life! It was her triple environment. It is also ours.

IV.

The Rain of Righteousness

~~~~~~

Text: *"It is time to seek the Lord, till he come and rain right-eousness upon you."*—HOSEA 10:12.

THE prophets of Israel lived close to God, close to the people and close to nature — three characteristics that every minister may well covet. From their communion with God they gathered inspiration, from their connection with the people they gleaned information, while from nature they drew illustration.

When Hosea spoke to the people, his words had about them a certain down-to-the-earth simplicity and vividness. "Israel," he cries, in the first verse of our chapter, "is an empty vine." His listeners know what he means, for vineyards are a large part of their stock in trade. "An empty vine!" It is probably in the reign of Jeroboam II, and the people are materially prosperous but spiritually poor. In the eyes of God they are "an empty vine" — green and luxuriant at a distance but barren of fruit when closely inspected.

In connection with our text the prophet uses a combination of figures drawn from the life of those who till the soil. He speaks of "fallow ground" — ground that has lain for long, unploughed, neglected, fruitless. It is baked hard by the sun perhaps, or overrun with weeds and thistles, or underlaid with a confused network of roots sent down by the virgin forest. That, says Hosea, is the heart of the people of Israel after long neglect of the house of God and the altars of true prayer and the ways of righteousness.

Then he calls for the clearing and the ploughing of this land: "Break up your fallow ground, for it is time to seek the Lord."

Now the field is ready for seed. So the prophet goes on to urge: "Sow to yourselves in righteousness." That is, do the things that a righteous God is requiring of you after these years of shameful idolatry and stubborn rebellion.

Well and good, so far. But no farmer can hope for a crop unless nature in kindness furnishes moisture. As with soils, so with souls! No man can hope to pass from a life of moral weakness into a life of moral strength unless God in kindness touches him with power from Above. No man can forgive his own sins; no man can heal the wounds of his own conscience; no man can make good to the full on the promises given to himself, to his dear ones and to God. Hence the need — the absolute need — of this further word that the prophet gives us in our text: "Till he (the Lord) come and rain righteousness upon you."

The same thing can be said of our group life. Here we are, as professing Christians, gathered into congregations and the congregations into conferences, or assemblies, or synods, or conventions, as the case may be; and these larger units gathered in turn into denominations. God knows that in all of these groups we need a revival: a revival of the *essential* in Christianity, for there has been too much emphasis upon the trivial; a revival of the *evangelical,* for there has been too much of the skeptical and the humanistic; a revival of the *ethical,* for there has been too much inconsistency in conduct; a revival of the *sacrificial,* for there has been too much of ease and smug comfort and self-seeking.

Some of us dimly see this situation. Some of our church leaders, perhaps a few of our national leaders, see that the church is weak as a force in our American society. We are told that religion must play a larger part in the life of these United States or we shall fall to pieces, broken on the rocks of our clashing self-interests, our group rivalries, our class and party strifes, our sectarian jealousies and ambitions. We have conferences on evangelism, we have "retreats" for taking stock of ourselves as religious leaders, we have, occasionally, a "religious emphasis week," or a "week of dedication." But, by and large, nothing much comes of it.

Our trouble lies in our unwillingness to follow God's recipe for spiritual recovery and revival. We are too easy on ourselves. We are not yet ready to get on our knees and come clean with God. In short, we are not willing to "break up the fallow ground," sow the seeds of truth and then let the great Lord of Harvest "rain righteousness" upon us. We need seriously to face up to Hosea's message.

I.

Spiritual Recovery and Revival Require Man's Response to God's Call.

God treats us as intelligent and responsible beings. He asks for our obedient cooperation in the realization of His purposes of grace and blessing. His prophet gives Israel to understand that there will be no "rain" of righteousness unless there is first of all thorough preparation of the soil on which the showers are to fall. "I'll send the rain," says the dear good God in effect, "but you must get ready for it: break up your fallow ground."

Now what does this homely figure of speech say to us? Does it not tell us that, before Divine blessing is poured out, some things must be looked after that are not easy?

For example, the fallow ground of sheer *spiritual uncon-cern!* What about having that broken up? William James, the famous Harvard psychologist, once said that there are some people for whom religion was like a "dull habit," while there are others for whom it is like an "acute fever." Religion as "dull habit"! Honestly now, isn't that a pretty accurate description of the Christianity that a lot of us have? When, if ever, did our hearts catch fire while we were reading some passage of the Word of God and we felt as if we should like to shout for very joy? When did we let the Holy Spirit lead us out of the beaten track to call at some new door and sit down to share the meaning of Christ and His Gospel with someone who was a stranger to both? When did we feel the thrill of going beyond the gift of our dimes and quarters to the cause of Christian service, and really lay out an offering of our money that forced us to deny ourselves a little something? When did we feel like going to our minister and saying, "Pastor, that Sunday School class of mine! I love those boys, and it seems to me I cannot stand it until they all know Christ as their personal Saviour"?

Oh, this lifeless, sparkless, conventional easy-going Christianity! How it puts a pleased smile on the Devil's face and squeezes the red blood of disappointment out of the heart of the passionate Christ!

Or, think of the fallow ground of *sin unconfessed*. In chapter 6 God complains, through His prophet, that the people of Israel have "transgressed the covenant." They have, He says, "dealt treacherously against me." In chapter 7 the charge is given in a more detailed way: Israel has been guilty of lying, of hypocrisy, of compromise with the practices of the heathen about her. In chapter 8 it is bluntly stated that the people "have sown the wind, and they shall reap the whirlwind." Chapter 9 closes with the lament that Israel "did not hearken" unto God.

How can there be the falling of copious showers of mercy and forgiveness, argues the prophet, unless there is first a willingness to look these failures and evils straight in the face and call them by their right name? It is the jaunty, callous, and even mocking way in which we can talk about sin that reveals how far some of us are from the "rain of righteousness," and at the same time how urgently we need it.

A couple of wisecracking "funsters" were broadcasting recently. One was describing to the other a power-dive in an airplane and what it felt like: "We dove down 30,000 feet, and all my sins flashed before me. It was so interesting I made the pilot go back and dive eight times more." The stooge, of course, is rocked with laughter, the studio guests joining in, and, presumably, plenty of the members of the listening audience. Sin isn't our shame these days; it is our jest, the source-material for our merriment.

Don't expect any revival in our heart, or in our church, or in our community, until we are ready to do something more serious and more Christian than laugh at, or deny, or evade the wrong things that are in our lives. One day, not long ago, some of us received a telegram from President Edman of Wheaton College concerning the powerful revival that had swept over their campus. Later we learned some of the interesting particulars associated with that movement of the Holy Spirit. For one thing, there was prayer — prayer that was focused and fervent. On a Tuesday classes were suspended and group prayer services were held in many different rooms. Then came a sort of judgment day. (The Scriptures speak of the fact that "judgment must begin at the house of God.") After a Thursday morning message on confession of sin, one of the members of the college track team asked for permission to speak. He made his way to the platform and publicly asked forgiveness for leading the track team in a cross-country race on Sunday against the wishes and without the knowledge of the administration.

Quietly President Edman said, "If there are others who need to confess their wrongdoings, they may do so now." One after another, students arose to unburden their hearts and openly to declare their purpose to be right with man and right with God. There was confession of cheating, of unkind criticism against others, of trying to follow Christ and the world at the same time, of spiritual pride, of prayerlessness, and of coldness. Some were choked with emotion, but most of those who spoke were strangely subdued. Yet they were plainly stirred to the very depths — and utterly sincere. On two days of that week the public sessions lasted for several hours each, some students standing for two or three hours waiting their turn to speak.

+ Here, you see, is something fresh from the life of our day that corresponds to the figure of speech employed by Hosea centuries ago. It is breaking up the fallow ground! It is discovering afresh that spiritual renewal and revival always come along the line of man's response to God's call.

If America wants revival, she can have it. If the Church wants a revival, she can have it. If you want a revival in your own heart, you can have it. But let us all remember that we can never have it on any other terms than those which God has laid down: the confessing and the forsaking of all known sin. You can pull wires and get something from the politicians, but not from God. His word to us is plain: "Let the wicked forsake his way and the unrighteous man his thoughts; and let him return unto the Lord, and he will have mercy upon him, and to our God for he will abundantly pardon."

II.

Spiritual Recovery and Revival Require Man's Reception of God's Gift.

How does a well ploughed and thoroughly prepared field get its moisture when the showers begin to descend? The answer is transparently simple: it just *takes* it. The rain is a gift from heaven — literally so.

So it is with us in the matter of spiritual refreshment. We pray, we think, we search our hearts, we confess our feebleness of faith, our lack of brotherly love, our absorption with the petty things of life, our transgressions against the mind of Christ. Thus the channels of our souls are opened up and God has a chance to flood us with His grace and forgiveness and cleansing and power.

The point is that this coming of God to our souls, when the channels are unstopped, is His gift to us. He comes not because we deserve it — for we do not — but because we *need* it and because it is His nature to give it.

The rain of righteousness! Righteousness as a free bestowal upon unrighteous men who do, however, hunger and thirst for it. The figure is a sparkling one. It speaks of *freeness.* Nobody thinks of trying to *buy* rain. It is one of the many bounties poured upon us by the lavish hand of the Creator. It is likewise with God's righteousness which He offers to us in Christ Jesus. Turn to Romans 5:17 and you hear Paul say that "they which *receive* abundance of grace and of the gift of righteousness shall reign in life by one, Jesus Christ."

A derelict of a man, all hungry and ragged, was given a check by a business man, and was told to use it to get some food and clothes. Some days later the business man met him on the street. To his surprise the poor fellow was just as unkempt and hungry-looking as ever. Suspecting the worst, he accused the man of taking the money and spending it for drink.

"No," said the unfortunate man, "here I have the check with me, but when I went to the bank to get it cashed, I looked at my clothes and then at the well-dressed clerks within and I said to myself that they would never give me the money."

"But," said the business man, it is not your clothes or your worthiness that decides the question. It is my name on that check."

Would to God we all might realize that He has put His name on the promise to forgive our sins, and heal our backslidings, and purge our lives of their carnal dross and empower us by His Holy Spirit. His name is on the promise, and it is written in the blood of His dear Son. "Then will I sprinkle clean water upon you, and ye shall be clean. From all your filthiness and all your idols will I cleanse you. A new heart also will I give you, and a new spirit will I put within you. And I will take away the stony heart out of your flesh, and will give you an heart of flesh." See! It is the rain of righteousness — heaven's gift for earth's refreshing!

The figure of righteousness descending as the rain speaks not only of freedom but of *fulness.* One is reminded of that gloriously extravagant promise God makes through His servant Isaiah: "For I will pour water upon him that is thirsty and floods upon the dry ground" (Isaiah 44:3). If we Christians did but realize it, there is in Christ for every one of us an inward spirit of righteousness which goes far deeper than our conduct — it cleanses and controls our motives, our purposes, our attitudes toward life and toward others.

A woman of India, huge in size and fierce in her spirit, entered a religious shrine seeking relief from the tempest that raged in her heart. There she met a tiny mite of a woman, who was a happy, helpful Christian. The two somehow fell into conversation. The big woman listened with a mingling of awe and unbelief as the little lady told of the power of the Gospel to change things from within out. When she came to a pause, the listening woman said, "You don't know me. I have laid a curse upon my family in a fit of anger. How can that curse be lifted and that tempest within me be stilled? No, it won't work."

"Try it," said the little lady, with patient and persuasive insistence. She herself was a radiant example of how it did work. But the large woman went away, shaking her head. One week passed. Then a strange scene occurred in that same temple court. The huge woman was shouldering her way through the crowd, looking for someone. Soon she spied the object of her search. It was the same little Christian lady she had met the week before, and who frequently came here to witness for Christ. When the two came together, the big lady put her long arms around her tiny friend, practically lifting her clear of the pavement, and as she did so, she exclaimed, "It works! It works! I tried it. Someone slapped me in the face today and I didn't even want to slap back. Something within me has changed. It works!"

What a shower of God's love had fallen in that woman's soul. It was the rain of righteousness! And when a thousand or two of us around where we live have a similar experience of being deluged from Heaven, our community will know that a revival has come.

III.

Spiritual Recovery and Revival Require Man's Recognition of God's Time.

"It is time to seek the Lord"! There are those who seem to think that we should passively wait until some tremendous emotion sweeps us before we begin seriously to pray and to make a surrender of ourselves to Christ. There are Christian people who seem to have the notion that spiritual awakenings which affect large masses of people are freakish things that come only when God is in the mood to send them. From the standpoint of Scripture I should like to challenge that whole view of things. It is not in the Book, and it is not in the Book because it is not in the nature of God. God is always in the mood to blot out the guilt of confessing sinners. God is ever eager to pour the fulness of the Holy Spirit upon consecrated children of His. God is yearning with desire to send blessing upon His praying, believing Church.

The delay is not in God. It is in ourselves. It is time for *us* to seek the Lord. Our trouble is that we are not wholeheartedly bent on breaking up the fallow ground. We aren't sure we are ready to go all the way with Christ. We are trying to put God off with our good wishes, when He wants our wills. We need to stop dilly-dallying, and begin to seek the face of Almighty God.

"It is time to seek the Lord"!

It is time for *America* to seek the Lord. A usually reliable magazine, closing a recent sketch of one of the most powerful figures now wielding authority in our national life, said that his personal wants are few and fairly simple, as expressed by the gentleman himself. And what do you suppose those wants are? The answer is: Two tailor-made suits a year, a comfortable bed, three meals a day and a reasonable amount of good liquor! I can stand it for you to set me down as a soft-headed alarmist or a Puritan in twentieth century clothes, but what I cannot stand is for my own honored country to go on befooling itself into thinking that such leadership can ever make the United States strong where strength really counts or safe where safety means most. We need to stop and listen to Jesus, as He fixes those pure eyes of His upon us and says, "Why call ye me Lord, Lord, and do not the things which I say?"

It is time for the *Church* to seek the Lord. Our hands are not altogether clean. Our inside politics, our pride of position, our sectarian bigotries and jealousies, our comfortable way of picking others to pieces and enjoying our polite cannibalism, our unconcern about the crying needs of people out of Christ — it is all an indictment. We sorely need revival.

Then in Heaven's name let us have it! God's skies are bursting with blessing. Why do we not break up our fallow ground and receive the delicious drenching of His Spirit's power and peace?

V.

Playing in the Market Place

~~~~~~

Text: *"And the Lord said, Whereunto then shall I liken the men of this generation? . . . They are like unto children sitting in the market place, and calling one to another, and saying, We have piped unto you, and ye have not danced; we have mourned to you, and ye have not wept."*—LUKE 7:31-32.

JESUS was master of parable because He was master of life. "He knew all men," said John on one occasion; and then added, "He knew what was in man."

Welling up out of this amazing knowledge of human nature in general and of these Pharisees in particular, comes this sharp-edged criticism of the shallow unbelief of the men of His day. The criticism flashes with all the keenness of a burnished blade. It is as penetrating as it is picturesque. The burden of its complaint is that the men who rejected Him stood self-convicted of inconsistency and insincerity. They simply lacked moral earnestness.

I.

Consider, first of all, the *Distinction which our Lord Implies*. Put bluntly, it is the distinction between *childlikeness* and *childishness*. To anyone who knows the four Gospels it is clear that Jesus found in childhood a realm of loveliness and enchantment. He was fond of children; they were fond of Him. It might almost be said that Jesus made a hero out of the child. He declared, "Except ye become as little children, ye shall not enter into the kingdom of heaven." In prayer to the Father He exclaimed, "I thank thee that thou hast hidden these things from the wise and the prudent, and hast revealed them unto babes." Nor can we ever forget the scene in which He administered rebuke to His ambitiously quarrelsome disciples by setting a child in their midst and quietly announcing, "Whosoever therefore shall humble himself as this little child, the same is greatest in the kingdom of heaven" (Matthew 18:4). Open, eager, artless, unpretentious, trustful — that was the childlikeness which the Master extolled. I suppose we might call this the *idealistic* use of childhood for purposes of illustration.

In our text, on the other hand, we have a *realistic* view of children, particularly spoiled children, in which Jesus shows up the folly and failure of the Pharisees. The picture presented is as life-like as a "rumpus room" or a playground, the application as irresistible as a lawyer's logic. Hadn't these bearded old "show-offs" of the sanctuary seen it many a time — those groups of boys and girls that gather in the public square? For a time all goes smoothly, hilariously. Then trouble! "What's the matter, children?" you say to them. "Aw, they won't play with us," says an angry-voiced youngster, speaking for one group. "We will, too; you won't play yourself," comes the equally testy reply of the other group.

"We said, 'Let's play wedding. Micah can be the groom and Rachel will be the bride. You, John, can be the Rabbi and the rest of us will be groomsmen and bridesmaids.' But John said, 'No, I don't want to play wedding. That's too silly.' We said, 'All right, then, let's play funeral. I'll be the corpse, John can be the minister, Sam the undertaker and the rest can be pallbearers.' But they said, 'No, we don't want to play *that* — playing funeral is too sad.' "

And there they were, throwing their peevishness back and forth at each other, getting nowhere except into a mutually miserable deadlock. Then came the Master's application of the story — keen as a sword-thrust. Look at what you did with John the Baptist and his ministry. John lived alone with the wind and the hills. John was a kind of hermit-prophet, solemn, uncouth, rugged. He preached repentance until it seemd like Doomsday for outcasts and churchmen alike. When you Pharisees went out into the wilderness to hear him, he flayed you for your hypocrisy and pride. When he had a chance to preach before Herod, he was the same fearless evangelist of repentance, demanding a thorough-going clean-up of the moral corruption around the palace. And none of you liked it, neither Herod nor yourselves. You said, It's too much like a funeral. You turned John down with the contemptuous charge that he was possessed with a devil.

Following John, came the Son of Man. He was different. There was nothing of the monk or the recluse about Him. He entered into the common life of the people. He contributed to the genial atmosphere of feasts and added the grace of gladness to wedding festivals. If John's ministry was like a funeral, Mine is like a wedding. Yet you are guilty of rejecting both. You say that John, in his aloofness and rug-gedness, was "possessed by a demon." You say that I, in my friendliness and joyousness, am "a winebibber and a glutton."

Can't you see it? says Jesus in effect. You are like peevish and unreasonable children. It is all right for six-year-olds to prefer a world of make-believe to a world of reality, but when the practice is carried over into adult life, it becomes a thing "too pathetic to be a joke." You have substituted for the simplicity and openness of childlikeness at its best the fickleness, selfishness and stubbornness of childishness at its worst. You are simply playing at religion — and making a bad job of it.

Ah, yes, someone is saying, the Lord Christ *had* to talk like that to those people. They were Jewish Pharisees. But it's different today — we are Gentile Christians. Very well, I want you to listen to this, from one of the most widely read religious authors of our times:

"I believe that the greatest trouble in the churches today is that a high percentage of our people . . . are spiritually without the vital experience of Christ which is gloriously offered in the New Testament. . . . Their Christianity, in fact, is not the real thing, but a spurious substitute. It is not *alive*. Based not on surrender, but on compromise, it is a conventional and poor copy of the real thing. In their hearts they know it is a sham, for there is no power in it. . . . In their hearts they know it is a fake, and the pathetic illusion of reality is kept up by attendance at services, a dangerous anesthetic; or by hectic service on this committee or that, a dangerous drug; or by passionate discussion of this problem or that, so often a deep dugout."

Plain words, aren't they? And they are addressed not to Jews of two thousand years ago but to professing Christians in this twentieth century. Professing Christians who need to be stabbed by the truth into a realization of how easy it is just to play at religion!

II.

Consider, in the second instance, *the Development which our Lord Suggests*. By introducing this picture of unstable and stupid childishness Jesus hints at certain ideas which are left to us to develop.

For example, one may say, broadly speaking, that *children love self-expression better than self-discipline*. The psychologist says they are "egocentric" — their world revolves around themselves. If they remain that way, it will be too bad for them and too bad for society. The resulting clash will ulti-mately break them, and certainly it will damage society.

The ways in which this childish self-assertion manifests itself in adult life are innumerable. We see it in family squabbles: it's the old tug-of-war between "I will" and "You won't," with no intelligent and disciplined effort to "give and take."

We see it in the extreme exhibitionism of vanity and extravagance: when cosmetics and jewelry take more of our money (which is not really *ours*) than charitable and Christian causes, we are guilty of an infantile self-display that would have brought blushes to the faces of the early Christians.

We see it in the business of war: men and nations may disguise their selfishness in what clever ways they can, but wars come because men persist in playing the old game of grab and strut and strut and grab.

We see it in the childish bickering and name-calling of our economic groups: the whole thing seems to justify the strong words of the writer who has said, "Men have become as soft as the times in which they have lived. We still have life, liberty, and the pursuit of happiness for which our fathers often had to fight and die. Let us be honest, we who ever boast of our achievements, let us shout it from the housetops that we claim another championship, that of raising the greatest crop of cry-babies ever produced in the history of the world."

We see it again in personal self-pity: those who live perpetually in a "state of self-reference" simply can't "take it" without feeling sorry for themselves. They are like the woman who suffered a nervous breakdown because she kept harrying herself with large doses of self-concern. Everybody else was to blame for her difficulties. Everybody picked on her — so she thought. Even those who sought to change her attitude were believed to be persecuting her. Self-defense and self-pity were the pattern of her life — and she a brilliant, educated woman. Even when she said, "I am sorry," it was not a forthright and humble confession, but an indirect form of her self-pity. In one conference with a counsellor she did say, "Yes, I am sorry — sorry that I did not take better care of my health." Obviously she had never grown up, either psychologically or spiritually.

Education, of course, recognizes all of these problems and tries to do something about this instinct of selfishness which is the source of our worst ills in life. Let it be said, in truth, that education does succeed generally in achieving certain results. As a minister of the Gospel, however, I should like to point out the distinction between what education does and what Christ does to break down this vicious circle of egocentricity. Let me employ a figure of speech. The child makes self the center of its life circle. Education comes along and says to that child, You must learn to get along with others, to respect their rights as well as your own, to serve their interests as well as yours. The effect is to change the circle into an ellipse — a circular figure with two centers. One center is "self," the second center is "others." That is an improvement, to be sure. The trouble is that it rarely, if ever works out in actual living, particularly when any strain is laid upon us.

Now what does Christ propose? He proposes to cure our childish ego-centeredness by a more radical procedure. He declares that this whole ellipse, with its two centers — "self" and "others" — must be caught up into a larger circle that includes the smaller. The center of this larger circle is neither "self" nor "others." It is "God." "Thou shalt love the Lord thy God with all thine heart . . . and thy neighbor as thyself!" And the good news is that this love toward God, transcending and sanctifying both our love of others and the proper love of self, is God's own gift to us. It comes as we surrender ourselves to it, with no holding back.

"Playing in the market place!" There is another development of this figure that comes to one's mind. Just this: It is a mark of infantile or childish acting to *prefer fiction to truth and romance to reality*. In his essay on *Shelley,* Francis Thompson says, "Know you what it is to be a child? . . . It is to be so little that elves can whisper in your ear: it is to turn pumpkins into coaches, mice into horses, lowliness into loftiness, and nothing into everything." Quite so! It is a stage of the game and, in its place, a charming one. But what happens to the child who does not learn the difference between this world of make-believe and the world as it is? Somewhere there will be a crack-up!

Now I want you to carry this problem to a still higher level. Let me put it this way: just as boys and girls like to "make believe" that pumpkins are coaches and mice are horses, so there are people who call themselves grown-ups who "make believe" that coaches and horses, and the things they represent, are all there is to life. They call it realism when, in point of fact, it is the most disastrous sort of romancing — a costly way of fooling ourselves.

Jesus pictured it for us in the parable of the Rich Fool. He had broad acres, fat crops, bulging barns — and a shrivelled soul. He tried to "sell" his soul on the idea that material possessions make life worth while: "Soul thou hast much goods laid up for thyself. Take thine ease: eat, drink and be merry." Goods! Goods! Goods! None of this church stuff for him! All of this twaddle about prayer and love and service and heaven — that's for Sunday School children and sentimental women! He was a realist!

Let's see whether he was or not. Came a night when death knocked at his mansion door. Death! Something he had never seen with his naked, greedy eyes! Something he couldn't weigh on those scales of his that he used for marketing his produce! Something he couldn't calculate on those well-filled ledgers of his! And then God! God stepped into the picture. Of course He had been there all the while — only the poor fellow, with coins over his eyeballs, neither wanted

61

Him nor recognized Him. After all, he was a realist. Yes, God broke in. And it wasn't pleasant either. That message from the Eternal had the tone of doom about it: "Thou fool, this night thy soul shall be required of thee: then whose shall those things be which thou hast provided?"

Children playing in the market place! Treating the ultimate facts of life as if they were fiction! And conversely, treating the perishable baubles of life as if they were eternal. His soul, you see, had plenty of sod but no sky. It had plenty of goods but no God. He was smothered by trifles, choked by the mere dust of life, with never a thought for its eternal meaning and its spiritual splendors.

It was this idea that came to arresting expression when, shortly after the bombing of Shanghai, Robert D. Abrahams wrote:

> *"Tonight Shanghai is burning,*
> *And we are dying too.*
> *What bomb more surely mortal*
> *Than death inside of you?*
> *For some men die by shrapnel,*
> *And some go down in flames.*
> *But most men perish inch by inch*
> *In play at little games."*

They perish — grown men and women that they are — because, like children fussing at their little games in the public square, they just played with life.

III.

Having observed the distinction our Lord implies (between childlikeness and childishness), and having traced out, in at least two particulars, the development of the figure He employs in the text, there is one thing more that should have our attention. I shall call it *the Demonstration that He Announces:* "But wisdom is justified of all her children," says the Master solemnly, searchingly, as in verse 35 the incident closes. The meaning, I think, comes out more clearly in the translation of Goodspeed: "So wisdom is vindicated by all who are really wise."

This wisdom of God, says Jesus, which was manifested in the ministry of John the Baptist, this wisdom which is being unveiled now in My ministry, may not be seen by you, because you are not dead in earnest; but it will appear — it will be demonstrated — to those who have spiritual insight.

Are we prepared — you and I — to face the meaning of that truth? Do we realize that the curse of trifling is blindness? If you are only playing at religion, the great and transforming energies of Christ's simple Gospel will never make any headway with you. If you are tilting at life casually, flippantly, making mock gestures with your pewter sword and your tin helmet, don't be surprised if Jesus Christ, and His precious blood, and the Church, and consecration, and selfless service, and heaven and hell, are strangely unreal to you.

If, however, life can somehow crowd you into a corner where you have to drop your mask of pretence and flippancy, if only you can be brought to the place where you are in earnest from the bottom of your soul about the things that really matter, then you will not treat Christ as a trifle or salvation as a jest. Then you will demonstrate for yourself the true wisdom of life: Christ the Saviour let into our lives to redeem them and Christ the Lord enthroned in our lives to govern them!

It was just such an experience of spiritual awakening that came to the young airman in the recent war when he wrote:

> *"Almighty and all present Power,*
> *Short is the prayer I make to Thee,*
> *I do not ask in battle hour*
> *For any shield to cover me.*
>
> *The vast unalterable way,*
> *From which the stars do not depart*
> *May not be turned aside to stay*
> *The bullet flying to my heart.*

63

> *But this I pray, be at my side*
> *When death is drawing through the sky*
> *Almighty God who also died,*
> *Teach me the way that I should die."*

No playing in the market place there! The wisdom and light of God, revealed through our Lord and Saviour Jesus Christ, had broken upon a soul that was dead in earnest. Has it broken on you?

VI.

The Fifth Freedom

〰〰〰〰〰〰〰〰〰〰〰〰〰〰〰〰〰〰

Text: *"If the Son therefore shall make you free, ye shall be free indeed."*—JOHN 8:36.

W E OF the United States, ever since our fore-fathers threw off the British yoke, have paid homage to the word "freedom." In recent years we have come to see that what we mean by freedom is difficult to maintain in one part of the world if it is denied in another part. So our public leaders, like our late President, have undertaken to broaden the base of political, cultural and religious liberty. They want freedom, as *we* understand it, extended to those parts of the world where it is not now enjoyed. With this in view they have turned loose in the world a phrase, a slogan if you will, that has become household property: "The Four Freedoms."

Freedom of speech and expression, freedom of worship, freedom from want, and freedom from fear — these, said Mr. Roosevelt in his now historic message to Congress, are rights that must be guaranteed to the peoples of the world. It is not my purpose to discuss these vital liberties. We all recognize them as being desirable. But I wonder if we are aware that they can never be realized in any large and permanent sense unless we add yet another freedom. It is that freedom of soul, that emancipation from selfishness and blindness, which Jesus Christ offers to men. This liberty is so basic to the other four that instead of calling it the Fifth we should be more accurate if we called it the First Freedom.

Jesus was a champion of freedom. He enjoyed it Himself. He wanted others to enjoy it. Yet everywhere He turned He found men who, in one way or another, were enslaved. Sometimes they realized it; sometimes they did not.

The men to whom Jesus was speaking in our text were, as a matter of fact, not well prepared to receive His teaching on freedom. Nor should we be too severe with them for that failure. We may fairly ask ourselves if *we* are ready to listen to Him — and respond. For if anything is certain, it is that Christ's freedom is far different from the notion that most of us have. Shall we try then to give Him a hearing as, quietly, penetratingly, confidently, He declares, "If the Son therefore shall make you free, ye shall be free indeed."

I.

Consider, first, the *character* of Christ's freedom as offered to us.

There are some things that you may quickly rule out. It is not freedom from *suffering*. The common ills of life do not cease to prey upon us when we give our allegiance to this Divine Master. Even He, faultless as He was, was not without pain. We all know that "painless dentistry" is something that exists only in the advertisements of second-rate dentists; we may be even more sure that there is no such thing as painless Christianity. "In the world ye shall have tribulation." Such is the forthright statement of the One who knows.

Then there is the fight with *temptation*. Christ's liberty does not exempt from that. His own life and example are full evidence: His freedom was not destroyed by His experience of temptation; it was rather enlarged. It is only when we surrender to the seducing power of wrong that we begin to lose our strength as free men.

Or, the obligation to respect and obey the requirements of God's law-abiding universe — this, too, is something from which Christ does not propose to loose us. He was not joking when He said, "I am not come to destroy the law but to fulfill it." The physical world and the moral world are alike in this, that they are ringed about and held together by laws so powerful that no fool and no knave can destroy them.

If some fool leaps from the twentieth story of a skyscraper, yelling his defiance at the law of gravitation, he doesn't break that law: he only illustrates it. By the same token exactly, if some knave goes out to steal or rape or murder, tossing his head recklessly at the commandments of God and society, he doesn't destroy the moral order: he only destroys himself against it. It is one of the pitiable delusions of our modern life that we are free only when we throw off all restraints or responsibilities and do as we jolly well please. That isn't freedom; it is bedlam. It isn't liberty; it is insanity. Far different is the freedom which Christ bestows.

Again, let it be said that Jesus does not guarantee *physical* freedom. To be sure, wherever in society His will is done and His spirit prevails, there men will not be coerced or enslaved or imprisoned. But that is the picture of an ideal order — an order of things that has never existed in this warped world of sinning humanity, nor does it exist today.

If Christ's freedom means anything for this life — and it certainly does — then it must be something we can possess *within* even when we are under force or pressure from *without*. Was Peter in prison Christ's free man? He was. Were Paul and Silas in the Philippian dungeon Christ's free men? They were. They were far more free than the jailer who fastened their aching feet in the galling stocks. Were the countless gallant souls who have hidden away in catacombs, who have been herded into the arena to be devoured by wild beasts, who have been fastened to the stake in order that their bodies might be fed to the torturing flames — have these men and women known anything that could possibly be called freedom?

Let the answer come from the lighted spirit of a noble French woman who during the years from 1695 to 1705 suffered for Christ's sake in several different prisons, including the notorious Bastille in Paris. I refer to Madam Guyon, whose intimate communion with Christ ranks her as one of the saints extraordinary. While she was in jail in Vincennes she wrote one of her most victorious hymns:

"*A little bird I am,*
  Shut from the fields of air;
Yet in my cage I sit and sing
  To Him who placed me there;
Well pleased a prisoner to be
Because, my God, it pleaseth Thee.

Nought have I else to do;
  I sing the whole day long;
And He whom most I love to please
  Doth listen to my song;
He caught and bound my wandering wing
But still He bends to hear me sing.

My cage confines me round;
  Abroad I cannot fly;
But though my wing is closely bound,
  My heart's at liberty.
My prison walls cannot control
The flight, the freedom of the soul.

Oh! it is good to soar
  These bolts and bars above,
To Him whose purpose I adore,
  Whose Providence I love;
And in Thy mighty will to find
The joy, the freedom of the mind."

There you have it: captivity of the body but liberty of the spirit!

I.

This brings us to the point of asking: What then is the positive *content* of the freedom which men are offered through Christ? We have eliminated certain things as not belonging essentially to this spiritual liberation. We therefore raise the question: What *does* belong to it?

For one thing, there is deliverance from what we may call the *bondage of the mind.* You will at once see why I use this phrase when I remind you of our Lord's statement just four verses removed from our text: "And ye shall know the truth, and the truth shall make you free" (v. 32). The bondage of the mind is the bondage of error, untruth, or, it may be, half-truth. How to be rid of *that* imprisonment is one of life's most urgent problems.

On this question of truth let us be quite clear that we are dealing with something wider and more significant than *facts*. Our age is fact-minded. No generation in all human history ever had such a dizzy mass of statistics at its disposal as our own. *Facts* have to do with the externals of life; *truth* has to do with its internal and eternal meaning and value. If I tell you that when a violinist plays his instrument he pulls horse-hairs across cat-guts, I am giving you facts, but I am by no means giving you the truth about the music of a violin. It is so with the nature of man or the nature of the universe. We have "clever" men, in some instances, trying to teach our young people in high school and college that man is simply a combination of so much lime, magnesium, potassium, sulphur, hydrogen, and so on. What they say may be within the facts, but the conclusions they draw may be as wide of the truth as it would be to say that a great painting is just pigment and canvas.

Without following further that line of contention, let's get right down to cases with these men in Jesus' day who first heard the words we are now seeking to understand: "Ye shall know the truth, and the truth shall make you free."

It was as though Jesus said to them, "You shall know the truth about *making your religion a reality,* and that truth shall make you free." Standing squarely in front of Him were men of sanctimonious countenance and distinctive garb who had the idea that God could be bought off with nice ceremonies and long prayers. To them Jesus would say, "Ye make clean the outside of the cup and platter, but the inside is full of ravening and wickedness." In other terms, live outside the temple the way you pray inside. *That* truth you need to set you free from something that is either useless formality or downright hypocrisy.

Or, it was as though the Master said, "Ye shall know the truth about *God and the largeness of His heart,* and that truth will make you free." Standing straight in front of Jesus were men who fancied that God had made the Jews His pets, and that He had little use, if any, for the unfortunate "dogs" who were to be classified as Gentiles. To them He would say, as He did to the Samaritan woman, "The hour cometh and now is when neither in this mountain nor yet at Jerusalem shall men worship God. For God is a spirit, and they (Jew, Samaritan, Gentile) that worship Him, must worship Him in spirit and in truth." Today, in many places the shoe is on the other foot: we Gentiles need the truth of God's universal love and pity, lest we remain under the deadly delusion that *we* are God's favorites to the exclusion of the Jews or anyone else.

Or, it was as though this Prince of Truth said, "Ye shall know the truth about *hatred and vindictive anger against your fellow-beings, and that truth shall make you free.*" Standing right in front of Him were men who lived by the rule, "Thou shalt love thy neighbor and hate thine enemy." Their hatreds had narrowed them, pinched them, seared them, as hatreds have a way of doing. That is not the way to live, said Jesus. God did not build you for hate, He built you for love. Hate enslaves; love liberates. It is this truth, among others, that I have come to plant in your hearts.

In this fashion Jesus Christ deals with the bondage of the mind and looses it from its blighting, cramping errors. "I am the light of the world," He cries (v. 12), "he that followeth me shall not walk in darkness but shall have the light of life."

Still, there is something besides the bondage of the mind that Christ deals with in His promise of freedom. It is the *bondage of the will.* Look now at verse 34, and note the solemn way in which the sentence begins, "Verily, verily, I say unto you, whosoever committeth sin is the servant of sin." I do not insult your intelligence by standing here and trying to prove to you that Jesus was right in that statement. The world is tragically full of folks who are walking, breathing illustrations of it.

You commit sin, and pretty soon sin will commit you — commit you to its own prison house. It has got you! Our acts of wrong so easily repeat themselves. Repeated, they become habits. As habits they become our masters, and we their unwilling servants. A few months ago, in the dead of winter, my young son touched a piece of icy steel with his tongue. The tip of the tongue froze fast. It was a bloody-mouthed but wiser boy who brought his tear-stained face into the house a few moments later. He was free to stick his tongue out, but he wasn't free to withdraw it. It hurt to keep it there and it hurt to pull it away. Thus it is when we trifle with dishonesties, immoralities and intemperances in our lives: so free to start; so helpless to stop!

"Helpless," did I say? Yes, and yet — blessed be God! — not helpless. In our lovely hymn, "Abide with Me," Christ is called "The Help of the helpless." He is just that! And I so present Him to you in this hope-filled moment. I do not say to you, who are held fast by habits that you yourself have come to loathe, "Try harder. Exert your will — what little you have left of it — a little more severely." That is neither good psychiatry nor good Gospel. Says one of our experts in mental and emotional problems, "The doctrine that the will alone is the way to power is a most woe-begone theory for the relief of the morally sick." No such "woe-begone theory" is it that I would offer to you now, but rather the simple, direct, inspiring challenge of Jesus Christ when He says, "Give me thine heart."

That is, stop thinking of yourself as a stagnant pool of poisoned water which *you* are vainly trying to purify, and begin to think of yourself as a channel through which God's forgiveness and healing and power will this moment start to flow if only you will really trust Him. The flow of His grace will put strength into your will, as it will put strength into every other part of your being. For,

> *"He breaks the power of cancelled sin,*
> *He sets the prisoner free;*
> *His blood can make the foulest clean,*
> *His blood avails for me."*

But there is still another aspect of deliverance which we must see if we would grasp the whole of Christ's message on freedom. The bondage of the mind is broken by the victory of truth over error. The bondage of the will is broken as the Christ Himself comes to us with God's forgiveness and love? Is that all? Not if I understand the Master correctly. There is, in addition, a promised deliverance from the *bondage of the spirit*. In this use of the word "spirit" I mean the desires, drives, and dispositions that lie back of our conduct.

After quoting the words, "Whosoever committeth sin is the servant of sin," Alexander Maclaren says, "That is true in two ways." What does he mean? One meaning we have already seen: repeated acts of sin become enslaving habits. But Jesus seems to have had something else in mind, along with this truth. If I practice a certain line of sin, I am advertising to the world that behind my conduct is an evil desire, an unholy sentiment, an indefensible disposition. What comes out is an expression of what lurks deeply within. And even after the practice has changed, the spirit of a man may be unsanctified.

A dip into real life will, I think, make the point reasonably clear. The late Dr. Charles Trumbull was once approached by a physician who wanted to get some assurance that he was living as a sanctified, triumphant Christian should live. It seems that a certain man had done the doctor a serious injustice. The doctor, in return, had been bitter.

Now he wanted Dr. Trumbull to know the situation was improved.

"You mean that you love him," said Dr. Trumbull.

"Well, I do not have that old bitterness I used to have."

"You love him then?"

"Why," said the doctor, "I am indifferent to him."

"Do you love him?" insisted Dr. Trumbull. Whereupon the man admitted, "I do not." Here was a case where a Christian was still inwardly enslaved by an old sentiment. The situation might have improved: at least the old doctor did not "see red" every time he laid eyes on his enemy. But — and I say this with emphasis — improvement is not victory. Nor is indifference perfect love — far from it. Jesus did not say, "Blessed are the indifferent in heart, for they shall see God." His word is, "Blessed are the pure in heart, for they shall see God." There, Christian, is your Emancipation Proclamation: the promise of a pure heart.

III.

Surely we want to know the *condition* on which we may be set free. "If the Son therefore shall make you free, ye shall be free indeed."

The simple truth is: Christ gives freedom by giving Himself. He is forever free, and where He is invited to come there liberty has its home and its happiness. Look at verse 35: "The servant abideth not in the house forever: but the Son abideth forever." That is to say, the servant or slave of sin does not need to remain forever in the house of sin. Why? Because the mighty Son of God, who dwells forever in the house of God's righteousness and love, will take a sin-bound man by the hand and lead him out into the glorious liberty of the children of God.

Henry Drummond, riding on the driver's seat of a public coach, was working with his usual, prayerful skill to win the coachman to Christ. The man's reluctance to surrender was due to his fear that a certain habit by which he was bound, would not permit a free and permanent decision.

"Suppose," said Drummond, "that your horses ran away and you lost control of them as they raced down a steep hill. What would you do?" The man confessed that he would be helpless. "But suppose," said Drummond, "that someone sat by your side who was really stronger, more skilled, than you are. What would you do?"

"I should give him the reins," came the quick reply of the coachman.

"Of course," said Drummond. "And your life has got out of control. It is running away with you. Jesus Christ, stronger than you, because He is God, asks for the reins of your life. Turn them over to him." He did it, and became a transformed man!

Drummond was letting him in on the secret of a life made free when he gave him the simple challenge I now give you: Turn over the reins to Jesus Christ!

VII.

"Now the God of Peace"

~~~~~~~~~~~~~~~~~~~~~~~~~~~~~~~~~~~~~~

Text: *"Now the God of peace be with you all. Amen."*
—ROMANS 15:33.
"The God of peace shall be with you."
—PHILIPPIANS 4:9.

COMMONLY, when the Bible speaks of God it is by the simple use of His name: just "God," without the article. As exceptions to this rule, however, we have a group of phrases in which He is described more explicitly as *"the* God" of this or that. Thus we read that He is "the God of Israel," "the God of hosts," "the God of heaven," "the God of all the earth," "the God of patience," "the God of all grace," and, as one of the most appealing titles of all, we have the designation which appears in our text — "The God of Peace."

Perhaps you think the preacher is either very daring or very dumb who, in tortured times such as these, attempts to speak on a topic like this. If so, may I say, quite frankly, that it is your *doubt,* and not the preacher's *daring,* that needs to be corrected. Our trouble is that most of the time we are afflicted with near-sightedness. Our vision lacks horizons. Our feelings move in the small circle of immediate circumstances. We forget that Hitlers are for a day; God is forever. And always, whether men are fighting each other or fawning upon each other, *He* remains "the God of peace." By which I mean that His supreme, unceasing, and final purpose for His creatures and His world is not discord but harmony.

Exactly this was the faith of St. Paul and the early Christians. Does anyone suppose that they were not being realistic when they spoke glowingly of "the God of peace"? Does anyone imagine that they were able to coin such a phrase as this, and find comfort therein, because they lived in a tranquil and untroubled world? Upon the contrary they waded through waters so deep and so dark that, on one occasion, Paul declared, "Our flesh had no rest, but we were troubled on every side; without were fightings, within were fears." Where, we might ask Paul, where was "the God of peace" during those harrowing hours? And Paul answers with one of those fine in-spite-of phrases which light up the New Testament. "Nevertheless," says he, "God, who comforteth those who are cast down, comforted us." So, chin-deep in difficulties, they still had experiences of the unfailing God who, through the lips of Jesus, says, "Peace I leave with you, my peace I give unto you; not as the world giveth give I unto you. Let not your heart be troubled, neither let it be afraid."

Now what happens when the whole of our life is given over into the hands of God? What does He then become to us? I propose that we seek an answer by tracing out the truth which gathers about three passages in the New Testament in which we find the expression, "the God of Peace."

I.

Take Romans 15:33 — "The God of peace be with you." Here God is presented as *the Presence Who Calms Us.* Let philosophers wrestle with the *idea* of God, and theologians with the *attributes* of God, and scientists with the *works* of God; but as for plain people, interested in the inner and sustaining vitality of true religion, nothing can satisfy them short of the realized *presence* of God. It is this *realization of the Presence* that Jesus came to make possible to men in a new way. He came to put vividness and beauty and strength and assurance into the experience. He came that, after having revealed God in utter love and in redeeming grace, He might say to men, "Lo, I am with you alway, even unto the end of the age."

The pity is that we read those words — too many of us — and they mean little more than so much printer's ink on a piece of white paper. Such a remark is not exactly gentle, I know, but before you resent it, be courageously honest with yourself. Is God real to you as an actual, living, loving, guiding, understanding and upholding presence in your life? Have you been introduced to Him the Jesus-way? By which I mean, have you come face to face with Him in Christ, as the One who has convicted you of *your* sins, as the One to whom you have confessed *your* sins, and as the One from whom you have received the priceless boon of assurance that *your* sins have been forgiven? Do you honestly know what the early Christians meant when they testified, "Therefore, being justified by faith, we have peace with God through our Lord Jesus Christ"?

More than that, do you do what that famous old saint, "Brother Lawrence," said that he did amid the pots and pans of the monastery kitchen: do you daily "practice the presence of God"? Do you know what it means to converse with Him as a friend — a friend who sits down with you, so to speak, in the silent shrine of your own inmost soul and imparts to you the power and glory of Heaven for the tasks and turmoils of earth? Do you know what the Bible means when it says that "Enoch (who lived, by the way, in godless days) walked with God"? Or what Paul means when he declares, in the howling of the tempest and the shivering of the doomed ship on which he rode, "There stood by me this night the angel (Christ) of God"?

If your heart has its glad affirmations in reply to these questions, then you know, in the Christian sense, what peace means in this trouble-torn world. You know that it doesn't mean coziness: it means confidence. It doesn't mean ease:

it means adequacy. It doesn't mean a delicately poised comfortableness: it means a divinely proffered companionship. It doesn't mean uninterrupted health, wealth, and prosperity: it means an unfailing inner strength, renewal and resiliency.

Troubled heart, baffled soul, there is a message here for you. The God of peace, of whom I speak, is not so named because He sits in some high, solemn and detached way, gazing down upon you and saying coolly, "This is good for you, this suffering that has smitten you like a thousand fiery arrows." That is a heathen's conception of deity. You get it in Tennyson's poem, *The Lotus-Eaters,* where the gods are described as aloof from the ills of the world:

> *"For they lie beside their nectar, and the bolts are hurl'd*
> *Far below them in the valleys, and the clouds are lightly curl'd*
> *Round their golden houses, girdled with the gleaming world:*
> *Where they smile in secret, looking over wasted lands,*
> *Blight and famine, plague and earthquake, roaring deeps and fiery*
> *   sands,*
> *Clanging fights, and flaming towns, and sinking ships, and praying*
> *   hands."*

And some folks, I fear, have thought that God is like those carefree divinities of the pagan mind. But He isn't. Put that in bold type: HE ISN'T! How do I know it? Because one day — and countless days since — I saw with unveiled eyes a Cross. Upon that Cross I saw the form of One tortured and twisted in a crimson sacrament of pain, suffering for no wrong of His, but for love of those who slew Him. From those lips I heard words impossible to doubt: "He that hath seen me hath seen the Father." And there — there as nowhere else in all the world — my soul found its answer to those who would tell me that God is too great, or too distant or too infinite, or too something, to be concerned about my troubles. There, at Calvary, I gathered boldness to shout back, "You are mistaken! God is not an absentee Sovereign who lives above and beyond the aches and ills of life. He is not outside of my tears and losses and sorrows: He is within them. He is within *them* because He is within *me,* sharing my else crushing load, guiding my stumbling feet, and reaching up to tear at least some tiny hole in the low-hanging cloud that through it might dart one bright beam of the eternal hope."

My colleague, Pastor Cabot Johnson, told a group of us the other night about a chap who enrolled as a freshman at Wheaton College. One day, when he was asked what he missed most during his first year away from home, he said, "At our house it is the custom for the whole family to stand around the table after breakfast and engage in family prayers. We form a circle by holding hands. For years," said he "I have stood next to my father, and again and again I have found that when Dad reached a particularly important point in his prayer, a point where perhaps he was talking to God about me, he would squeeze my hand. Now that I am away from home, I think that of all the things I miss, the one that I feel most keenly is the pressure of my father's hand every morning."

Fortunate is the young man who has such a father! Yet circumstances brought that young man to the place where the father's hand could not reach him. That human limitation makes all the more welcome the news I bring you now: There *is* a Father whose ear is never heavy and whose hand is never shortened. And His name is "the God of peace," because, when His children are lonely and bereft and pain-wracked, it is the gentle pressure of His hand that tells of His presence. What more could they ask?

II.

The God of Peace as *the Purifier Who Cleanses Us.*

We turn now to I Thessalonians 5:23, where we read, "And the very God of peace sanctify you wholly; and I pray God your whole spirit and soul and body be preserved blameless unto the coming of our Lord Jesus Christ." In the Christian sequence of things surely it can be said that our second point follows naturally and logically upon the first. If we have the presence of the God of peace, we simply cannot escape the issue of holiness.

The practical question is this: How far are we Christians prepared to go with God (or should we say, how far will we let Him go with us?) in making something clean and lovely and Christlike out of us? Do you really long to be free from sin, to have a *self* that is fundamentally organized and unified around the mind of Christ that possesses us? There are too many of us who sing hymns about longing "to be perfectly whole" when we are glib and shallow about it. When it comes right down to it, we are not ready to give up our right to ourselves, or part company with every attitude, habit, and disposition that contradicts the spirit of Christ, or lay on the altar, once and forever, all the capacities and possessions which we call "ours" but which are really God's.

When it comes right down to it, we find our carnal, unsanctified hearts siding in with the creeds of men more than with the words of Holy Scripture. We read in one of the historic catechisms, "No man, even by the aid of Divine grace, can avoid sinning, but daily sins in thought, word and deed," and we go for that because it gives generous comfort and leeway to the worldly, wayward, and selfish urges within us that we have never allowed Christ to deal with.

Or perhaps we go off balance at another point, and conjure up false notions of what it means to be wholly sanctified as a follower and friend of Jesus Christ. We tell ourselves that people who go in for sanctification usually end up by professing that they have reached a place where they are never tempted — a claim, incidentally, that very few fanatics have ever made. Or, there is that related bogey which frightens us — the teaching that sanctification means the impossibility of committing sin. It doesn't, of course. And extremely few have been the deluded souls who ever dared to say that it does. But there is an unholy devil who makes it his unholy business to keep these skeletons dangling before the fearful eyes of Christians who really should know their Bible well enough to know better.

What I have found, in reading and praying over my New Testament is that there is a definite and decisive sanctification of the Christian's heart and there is a daily sanctification of the Christian's life. Both are in the mind of St. Paul in the passage which is before us. "The very God of peace sanctify you wholly." Weymouth renders it, "make you entirely holy." The verb is in the Greek tense called the aorist: a ministry of cleansing that is decisive and thorough! That is the sanctifification of crisis, in which the Christian has an *encounter* with his Lord.

Then the apostle adds, "and I pray God your whole spirit and soul and body be preserved blameless unto the coming of our Lord Jesus Christ." And that is the sanctification of process: the daily yielding of our cleansed being — the whole of what we are as redeemed men and women under the Lordship of Christ — to God's will and service. This daily yielding, moreover, includes the humble recognition and confession of our shortcomings and infirmities.

But mark you, if you want to make a success of the sanctification of daily process, you will need to make sure of the sanctification of definite crisis. Somewhere God must be allowed to uncover the unsightly and unseemly depths of your self-life. Somewhere there must be a revelation of the deeper meaning and power of the Cross of Christ, with its uncompromising message: "Except a corn of wheat fall into the ground and die, it abideth alone: but if it die, it bringeth forth much fruit."

Some months ago I received a letter from a father and mother whose daughter, in her late teens, had attended a school where I had spoken. They wanted me to know about the triumphant death through which the daughter had just passed. She had gone to this college as a young Christian, but, like so many Christians, without a personal, practical realization of Christ's ministry of cleansing and victory in the life. In a series of revival services on the campus she had made her full dedication and had experienced Christ as her sanctifying Lord. Among her papers, so the parents wrote, they had found this prayer of confession and consecration that had come from her burdened heart at the time of her spiritual crisis:

"God, You know how empty and aimless this life has been and You know the fruitless hours I have spent on myself and my own interests. I don't know why You still love me, unlovely as I am, but I know you do, for You have said, 'I have loved thee with an everlasting love.' Lord, I want You to be my Lord; take this stubborn, hateful life and live through me. I made a mess of everything, but, please, God, take me; I'm Yours for whatever You want to do with me. If You take away everything that I hold dear, give me the patience of Job, the faith of Abraham, but above all, the love of Christ. This is my heart's prayer."

So remarkably was that prayer answered that her father and mother were able to write of the new radiance and power that entered her life and characterized the last months of it: *"She laid all on the altar and from that time grew spiritually by leaps and bounds. . . . She studied her Bible and memorized Scripture until many marvelled at her insight. . . . During her last night she rose up in bed and shouted, 'The victory is won.' "*

For her, you see, "the God of peace" had become both the Presence who calms the soul and the Purifier who cleanses it.

III.

The God of Peace as *the Perfecter Who Commissions Us.*

We pass next to Hebrews 13:20, 21, where we read, "Now the God of peace . . . make you perfect in every good work to do his will, working in you that which is well pleasing in his sight." What is the Christian's business in this world? Is it to revel comfortably in God's love? Yes, but that is far from all of it. Is it to rest securely in the sense of one's own salvation? Yes, but that cannot be the whole of it. Is it to contemplate with fascination the glory that awaits us beyond the shadows? Yes, but more.

According to this apostolic benediction our business is to be the commissioned servants of God's will! To *do* His will! That is the thing for which there is no substitute. To this end Christ has redeemed us. For this purpose He became "our bleeding Sacrifice." For this reason He rose from the dead. Unto this objective our hearts have been "perfected," that is, adjusted to, harmonized with, the heart of God.

> *"He wills that I should holy be,*
> *That holiness I long to feel,*
> *That full, divine conformity*
> *To all my Master's blessed will."*

Only as we come into such vital accord with God's purpose can we be useful to Him in full measure.

But even then we are running headlong into difficulty. What though the service we render shall come from a heart of utter devotion, the service itself, we painfully realize, is a frail and awkward thing. Can there ever come of it that which is worthy of God? Besides, there is the pitifully short time we have in which to perform it. A few years that fly with breathtaking speed, and the tasks we barely began must be dropped by our palsied hands! Isn't it a depressing and hopeless business, after all — a vast and inescapable frustration?

Think of Cecil Rhodes, Africa's brilliant and tireless explorer and developer — one of the most prodigious toilers of the nineteenth century — facing death at less than fifty, and saying regretfully, "So much to do, so little done." Think of the countless ones in the long march of the centuries who have felt that death has claimed them when the record of achievement was such a meager one, when indeed the temptation was strong upon them to feel that they had failed.

Had they failed? Not for one hour — not if they had lived their lives under the commission and control of the God of peace. For, cries the apostle, to all such workers in the blessed kingdom of God's will, He is "working in you that which is well pleasing in his sight, through Jesus Christ, to whom be glory forever and ever." Ah, that is a great word on which to end — He Himself is the completion of every unfinished task. He Himself is the beautifier of every clumsy product of our willing but unskilled hands. He Himself guarantees that the projects on which we have worked with so little success in time will be carried over into fadeless fruition in eternity.

VIII.

A Christian's Three Loves

Text: *"Thou shalt love the Lord thy God . . ."*
"Thou shalt love thy neighbor as thyself."
—MARK 12:30, 31

ONE of our carefree modern poets, whose delight
it was to shock people, wrote an odd-sounding couplet which
goes like this:

"There's nothing in any religion
Which compels us to love the pigeon."

Whatever Ogden Nash meant by these lines, they do raise
two important questions: first, can you call anything "love"
if it is *compelled,* if there is a "Thou shalt" in front of it;
and, second, just what is it that our Christian religion
requires us to love?

The second of these questions is what concerns us chiefly
in this message. The first one, however, needs to have some
clearing up, it seems to me, if we are to get on well with our
discussion of what a Christian is to love.

"Thou shalt love"! Break off just those three words. It
doesn't sound right, does it? "Thou shalt" is a command.
It sounds like a direct appeal to the will, which in one sense
it is. But love is of the heart, we say. Love is an emotion.
You can command the will, but how can you command the
heart? We find ourselves asking, sincerely enough, who would
want to put up with someone's *forced* love? If he was told

85

that he *had* to love me, how much could I value that sort of affection?

How, then, does Jesus want us to understand Him when He says, "Thou shalt" love God . . . "Thou shalt" love thy neighbor . . . "Thou shalt" love thyself? I shall make only two observations, which to me, however, go far toward clearing up our difficulties. The first is this: that in the Christian religion the believer stands so related to Christ that Christ's commands never come to us as bare commands, standing alone; they rather come to us as *implied* promises. The Lord Jesus Christ never asks the impossible. To be sure, He often asks the *humanly* impossible, since there is no meaning in His mission as the Divine Redeemer if He does for us no more than we could do for ourselves. Here indeed is the critical point where the glory of the Gospel blazes out: Christ asks for more than we can supply and then proceeds to furnish the difference Himself. It was Augustine, I believe, who once prayed, "O God, give what Thou commandest, and then command what Thou wilt."

If, then, we are commanded to love, it is only because God offers us the gift of His own Holy Spirit to enable us to fulfil the requirement. Thus in Charles Wesley's great hymn, *Love Divine, All Love Excelling,* we sing:

> *"Jesus, Thou art all compassion,*
> *Pure, unbounded love Thou art;*
> *Visit us with Thy salvation,*
> *Enter every trembling heart."*

The second observation follows. It is that love, in the distinctly Christian sense, does indeed bear a much closer relation to the *will* than one might suppose. The plain truth is that we have no very good English word for the Greek term that is translated "love" in such a passage as we have before us. Our word "love" is overloaded. We try to make it carry too many meanings. It is what a toiling mother gives her child, but it is also what a four-times married Hollywood

actress is supposed to give to a three-times divorced Hollywood actor. It is what that dear couple give to each other
when, with hair of silver and heart of gold, they celebrate
a half-century of marriage, but it is also that unhallowed
thrill of a night's "petting" party. Which reminds us that
some of the qualifying adjectives we sometimes associate with
love are themselves a confession of the poverty of our mother
tongue at this point. We hear, for example, of "puppy love,"
concerning which someone has said that it is often "the beginning of a dog's life!" Quite so.

What I am pleading for now is that we look at this New
Testament word for love from a new angle of vision. We
need to see it high above the coarse muck of careless passion,
high above the soft ooze of mere sentiment and emotion, yes,
even above the passing moods of spiritual exhilaration. We
need to see it — and this is the point I wish to emphasize —
as *active good will*. It is of the very nature of God. Indeed
it is so described in the story of God's gift to us in Jesus
Christ: "peace on earth, good will toward men."

Let's apply it to these three commands of Jesus which are
before us, and see where we come out.

I.

We shall begin with the third one and work back to the
first. In such an arrangement we are confronted with *the
love which we owe ourselves*. That startles us, but it is the
teaching of Jesus nevertheless. "Thou shalt love thy neighbor
as (in like manner) thou shalt love thyself." There can't
be any mistaking of the Master's meaning. Paul writes to the
Christians at Ephesus regarding the Christian view of marriage, and says, "So ought men to love their wives as their
own bodies," or, as the Weymouth translation has it, "So too
married men ought to love their wives as much as they love
themselves."

I can well imagine that this is confusing to some of us. Perhaps there are those who have heard this preacher talking about the evil and mischief of the "self life" and the Christian necessity of our being dead to self. And now they hear the preacher declare that self-love is actually one of the commands of Christ.

Well, the contradiction is only on the surface. If Christian love is active good will, patterned after God's will toward us, then self-love is a very different thing from self-centeredness, or self-glorification, or self-wilfulness. Self-love is what I should call a healthy respect for our own soul. Individual manhood, individual womanhood — there is nothing else like it in all this mysterious world. It is the handiwork of God. It may be marred and battered; it may be warped and wicked; it may be saintly and splendid; it may be gifted and gracious. In any case it is the contrivance of the Eternal Wisdom. Deity is stamped upon its faith. Eternity beats in its blood. Destiny waits upon its movement. This being so, I had better treat it with good will, with intelligent regard, with unceasing concern.

It is this self-love perverted that causes all our troubles — from international conflicts to family squabbles. Someone has said that "self is a glorious servant but a gruesome master." When we love ourselves as the servants of God and of His creative purposes, all is well. When we love ourselves as the lord and master of everything we survey, we invariably manage, sooner or later, to fashion an intolerable hell for ourselves — a wretched hell *here* before ever we reach the one that waits hereafter.

> *"I gave a little tea party*
> *This afternoon at three.*
> *'Twas very small, three guests in all,*
> *I, myself, and me.*
> *Myself ate up the sandwiches.*
> *While I drank all the tea;*
> *'Twas also I who ate the pie,*
> *And passed the cake to me."*

About the only difference between that kind of hell and the one that lies beyond is that from this one there *is* a possibility of escape. If you ask how, I answer: The same way the prodigal used!

You remember his story, as told by the Master. That prodigal made two prayers, according to Jesus, and between them there lies a world af difference — the difference between false self-love and true self-love. Both prayers may be boiled down to two words. First, "Give me!" "Father, give me the portion of goods that falleth to me." He and his own interests were at the center. They dominated everything. Result? First, disappointment. Then disgust. Then complete disillusionment.

What followed was redemptive: "He came to himself!" Self-centeredness — this perverted self-love — is a form of insanity. It always turns, like the Sirens of Ulysses' day, and rends the victims of its deceptive music.

Now the second prayer: "Make me!" Not "Give me," but "Make me!" "Father, make me as one of thy hired servants." Mind you, self was still in the picture, for we can never escape ourselves. But what a different self — humbled, broken, usable. We need that healthy regard for our own soul, or life will go competely to pieces and be forever wasted.

II.

Consider, in the second place, *the love we owe our neighbor*. "Thou shalt love thy neighbor!" "As thyself!" Martin Luther has a comment on these words that is as choice and charming as any tapestry. "We give this rule," says he: "The good things that we have from God ought to flow from one to another, so that every one of us may as it were put on his neighbor and so behave towards him as if he were himself in his place. As our heavenly Father has freely helped us in Christ, so ought we freely to help our neighbor and each should become to others a sort of Christ; that is, that we may be truly Christians."

Take up this word "neighbor" a moment. It is an extremely timely word for us just now. You remember that when Jesus introduced it in the parable of the Good Samaritan, it was in reply to a quibble that the lawyer had raised over the definition of the word. The lawyer had his own smug, shrunken definition. A neighbor? Why, of course, that is my friend next door, who belongs to the same race and color that I do; to the same social set that I do; perhaps even to the same business and religious group that I do. If *he* gets in trouble, I'll be right there to serve him in any way I can.

Oh, no, said Jesus, that definition is far too small and selfish. Your neighbor is anyone, anywhere, "whom circumstance puts it in your power to befriend." If you use this power, you may be said to "neighbor" him. The example given was exasperating to all human pride, prejudice and pettiness. The "neighbor," of all things, turned out to be a merciful Samaritan who showed no end of kindness to a despised Jew.

It occurs to me that this ancient quibble, which Jesus so drastically dealt with, no longer has even the pretense of justification which the lawyer could claim for it in that tightly divided little world of ancient Palestine. The old barriers of geography and state are gone. The boundaries that we now have are psychological, not geographical. It is sixty hours by plane from any local airport to any major landing field on the face of the globe. In a day when the nickel which we handle comes from New Caledonia and the linoleum on which we walk may have in it raw materials from fabulous, far-away Afghanistan, the whole world has become a neighborhood. We may like it or not like it. In either case it is a fact.

And one deduction from this tremendous contemporary development is that the cause of Christian missions in the world has taken on its deepest, widest meaning in all the Christian centuries. On the very day that Pearl Harbor was attacked a returned missionary to the Orient was met by an acquaintance of his who, with a leer in his eye and a jeer in his voice, said, "Well, what do you think of your Japanese now?" To which the missionary replied, as with the quiet thrust of a lance, "*My* Japanese are very well, thank you. I presume they are safely in bed. If you are talking about the ones that just bombed the American fleet, they are *your* Japanese. They are the ones you were too stingy to send the Gospel to!"

If we "love our neighbor as ourselves," we want peace. If we want peace, we must have Christian missions. The logic of it is inescapable. Nor is it any adequate reply if the cynic reminds us that Germany had had the Gospel for generations when she launched the world into war twice within the century. What the cynic needs to be reminded of is that neither the Prussians nor the Nazis could develop any dynamic or drive for their warfare of aggression until they had sabotaged the message of Christianity. Here is a sample from the teaching of an official Nazi text book: "*The teaching of mercy and love of one's neighbor is foreign to the German race, and the Sermon on the Mount is, according to Nordic sentiment, an ethic for cowards and idiots.*"

I can think of a good many reasons why American Christians should be concerned about the missionary enterprise, but I can think of none that is more immediately and inescapably obvious than this: we must evangelize with Christ or perish in World War III in the easily forseeable future.

III.

Think, finally, of *the love we owe to God*. And again I would make this, if possible, a practical and realistic message.

When our Lord says that we are to love God with all the "heart," the "soul," the "mind," and the "strength," He means, I take it, a total surrender of personality to God and to the carrying out of God's holy purposes. I put it this way, lest someone get the notion that he must always *feel* a warm glow of emotion toward God. No, our emotions, even where the high and holy God is concerned, are fluctuating. They rise and fall.

Meanwhile — and this is of the greatest importance — our abiding yieldedness of will and purpose remains unbroken and unchecked. We desire, above all things else, that His work shall succeed, that His kingdom shall prevail, that His Son Jesus Christ shall be enthroned in the hearts of men everywhere. This is our active good will towards the God Whom we trust.

To be sure, there will be a good deal of emotion bound up with this magnificent surrender to Him. There will be times when, in the language of Peter, we can say, "Whom having not seen, we love; in whom, though now we see Him not, yet believing, we *rejoice with joy unspeakable and full of glory.*"

Yet it will not always be so. To love God with our emotions when our sky is without a cloud and all the birds of summer are singing — this indeed is easy. But when the last glint of sunlight has faded from the scene, when some fierce and fatal storm has swept through your home, when disease and pain have seized your defenseless body and seem determined to break it, what about your love for God then? Ah, then is when you, as a Christian, can offer Him the love of good will. You believe that an infinite kindness resides in His heart, though you cannot for the moment appreciate the chastening through which His love for you is causing you to pass. You trust that His purposes, at least in the ultimate, are good and holy, and you want them to triumph. You say, with Job, "The Lord gave, and the Lord hath taken away: blessed be the name of the Lord." That is your love for Him cast in the noble mould of good will.

Years ago, at West Stanley, England, a mine explosion occurred. Scores of men were entombed, many of them were killed. That saintly and scholarly soul, Dr. Handley Moule, the bishop of Durham, was not far away. He journeyed over to the head of the mine, where he found a large crowd of anxious, stricken relatives and friends. He was asked to address them. What could he say? But they respected and honored him. He must give them some word as a Christian minister.

"It is very difficult," he began, "for us to understand why God should let such an awful disaster happen, but we know Him and trust Him, and all will be right." Then he went on: "I have at home an old book-marker given me by my mother. It is worked in silk, and, when I examine the wrong side of it, I see nothing but a tangle of threads crossed and recrossed. It looks like a big mistake. One would think that someone had done it who did not know what she was doing. But, when I turn it over and look at the right side, I see there, beautifully embroidered, the letters GOD IS LOVE. We are looking at all this today," he concluded, "from the wrong side. *Some day we shall see it from another standpoint, and shall understand.*"

Years later there were those who testified to the quiet comfort that came to them as the wise Bishop gave his simple message. The message is deathless. It is our salvation. It is our solace. It is our strength. It is this: God is love. Because He is love, He gave His Son to save us. Nothing, absolutely nothing, can rob us of that towering fact. We therefore love Him because He first loved us!

IX.

Are You Many or One?

Text: *"Unite my heart to fear thy name."*—PSALM 86:11.

RING almost any doorbell that you choose, and you will find someone in the house who is struggling with inner conflict and tension. We read in the Scriptures, "Thou wilt keep him in perfect peace whose mind is stayed on Thee," and yet few of us know what it means to live day by day in that zone of life.

To be sure, a certain amount of tension is unavoidable. We consist, for example, of body and spirit. The body has certain "drives," such as hunger, fear, sex. The spirit has certain impulses and ideals, such as conscience, reverence, and worship. Maintaining the ascendency and control of the spiritual on the one hand and the discipline of the physical on the other, is not always easy. When St. Paul declares, "I keep under my body," he is hinting surely of some sort of tension in his experience.

Or, take the conflict that is everywhere to be found between good and evil. Every decent man, and especially the man who has opened his heart to the saving grace of the Lord Jesus Christ, is a center of resistance against all of the forces of wrong that are loose in the world. From this point of view it is neither possible nor desirable that one should live without any sense of clash or conflict.

It is in another direction that our text asks us to look. "Unite my heart to fear thy name!" That is the cry of the man who knows how unhappy, unhealthy, and unfruitful is the life that issues from a divided heart. He is the man of double mind — partly for Christ, partly for self. He is the man of double will — partly surrendered, partly reserved. He is the man of double loyalty — partly to the kingdom of God, partly to the kingdom of this world. Such a man pleases neither himself nor his Lord. Such a man had better pray with the psalmist of yesterday: "Unite my heart to fear thy name."

I.

Consider more closely the Condition of a Divided Heart.

That it is a *real* problem in living requires no labored proof. So many of us are personal echoes of Paul's words in Romans seven: "The good that I would, I do not. The evil that I would not, that I do." The pity is that we haven't come to the place of desperation to which Paul came when he cried, "O wretched man that I am, who shall deliver me from this body of death?"

Said a young lady to me not long ago: "I know what I ought to do, but I am not sure that I want to do it." Divided — and therefore impotent! Another said, "I want to do it, but I don't want to enough to get it done — not enough to really say 'Yes' to God." Again, divided — and therefore unhappy.

Some months ago I walked out of a book shop with a little volume in which there occurs this pertinent sentence: "We are trying to live several selves at once, without all our selves being organized by a single mastering life within us." Thus a modern thinker speaks of a condition that David knew all about three thousand years ago. "Several selves at once!" "No single mastering life within!" How close those phrases come to describing the confusion, or at least the division, that exists within the kingdom of Mansoul.

The self that Christ is seeking to produce is a unified whole. It may not be a fully grown self, but it should be, and can be, a totally surrendered self. It is a self from which unworthy loyalties have been cleansed and in which all worthy but lesser loyalties have been gathered up in a sacrament of consecration to God, who must be forever the object of our supreme loyalty.

But here we are — many of us — bewitched and befuddled by the play of other selves that have never been really cornered and crucified. There's an *ambitious* self that just will not wait humbly on God for Him to reveal His plan for our life and define success for us as *He* wants to define it. It clamors for human applause, craves this world's goods no end, and would rationalize the use of shady methods to gain a coveted goal.

There is a *jealous* self whose feelings, always on the surface, are always being hurt by the unappreciative or slighting attitudes of other people; whose peace, moreover, is forever being molested by the achievements or the promotions that come to those with whom one associates.

There is an *angry* self that, more or less frequently, deserves to be arrested for "disturbing the peace." Only there seems to be no policeman around to do the arresting! And that Officer from Above, the Holy Spirit, who really could do the job — well, for some reason we simply do not make use of His services. So the peace continues to be disturbed — even for the neighbors at times!

Someone needs to do for us what a young minister did for a friend of his. The friend looked over the clergyman's shoulders and saw that he was writing on the subject, "Do We Really Want God's Control?" The friend, who was in many ways an earnestly religious man, said, "The answer to that question is 'No.'" Then he went on to point out the tight places in the Christian life where so many of us try to serve Christ and have our own way at the same time: giving way to the fear of other people's opinions, taking them in our own hands so as to insure the realization of some personal ambition (perhaps even for church office), being lazy about the business of the Lord and His Church, and all that sort of thing. When there came a pause, the minister said, *"All of us Christians must choose which pain we want to suffer: the pain of a crucified self, or the pain of a divided mind."*

He might have added that the pain of a "crucified self," though often bitter, yields an inexpressible joy: whereas the pain of a "divided mind," destitute of any compensating joy, travels its thorny trail to some precipice of collapse and doom.

II.

Consider next the Consequence of a Divided Heart.

We need, in this connection, to examine the whole verse of which our text is a part: "Teach me thy way, O Lord; I will walk in thy truth: unite my heart to fear thy name." The first two clauses, you see, are divided by a semicolon, but both of them are followed by a colon which introduces the clause of our text. Clearly then, it is the understanding of the translators that the prayer for a unified heart is offered in order that the psalmist might be taught God's way and, being taught it, he might walk therein.

The implications of such a prayer are not to be overlooked. The first one, let us say, is this: *a divided heart lacks perception.* It is all very well to say, "Lord, teach me Thy way;" but unless we also pray, "unite my heart, bring this inner confusion to an end," the light will not break in.

Some people sing hymns of consecration at the top of their voices but at the bottom of their hearts there are locked doors of reservation. Then they wonder (or say they do) why no more light comes to them on their problems. Jesus said, "If thine eye be *single*, thy whole body shall be full of light." A Christian woman, tormented and all but broken with

97

divided loyalties in her inner life, came to me for counsel and prayer. In the course of the interview I quoted those words of Jesus. Long afterward she said, "You know when you gave me that verse the first time, I couldn't grasp it. Now I realize what it means, and I realize how perfectly it fitted my case." "If thine eye be single," that is, focused on one object — God — then thy whole being will be flooded with His light. If you want God's will to be unfolded to you, you must be wholehearted in your desire for it and your willingness to embrace it. If you want your mind enlightened with God's Word, you must make sure that your heart is not at cross-purposes with that Word. To see truth clearly, you must be surrendered to it utterly.

Moreover, a divided heart lacks *power*. Listen to the psalmist again: "I will walk in thy truth" — and to this end, "Unite my heart." In the Scripture the Word "walk" signifies our practical living. In their profession of Christian manhood and womanhood, some people really walk for Christ, and others just wobble. But always the outer wobble is the sign of an inner weakness — a divided heart. The apostle James said it so well we cannot hope to improve upon the saying of it: "A double minded man is unstable in all his ways." God sees his double mindedness; the rest of us see the instability of his ways.

In the first World War the Allies tried the method of multiple control in the handling of their armies. It failed. Then they made Foch the generalissimo of all the forces, and they got somewhere. In this last war it was decided early that the invasion of Europe and its preliminary operations could be carried through successfully if, and only if, someone was placed in supreme command. That position, as we all know, was given to General Eisenhower. Where would the Allied cause be today if we had been subjected to the frictions, vacillations, hesitations, and indecisions that invariably grow out of multiple or divided control? The confusion would be hopeless.

The principle holds good on the more personal battle-field of your life and mine. Who is to have our unmixed and undistracted loyalty — Christ or Caesar? Peter's soul was a battleground that tragic night long ago when His Master was on trial. He was for Jesus, but not altogether. When the accusing damsel said, "Thou also wast with Jesus of Nazareth," he was a frightfully divided man. It was a trying hour, of course. The stand he was called upon to take looked so humiliating and difficult. In reality it wasn't difficult at all. If he had been committed, uncompromisingly and irrevocably committed, to loyalty and honor, if in other words he had not been a man of divided heart, the decision would have been simple. It might have been costly, but it would have been simple. But Peter, a man under dual control, has gone down in history as the man who denied his Lord. Behind him trails the testimony that a divided heart lacks power: power to do the will of God, power to walk in the way of courage.

Our context suggests a third thing with regard to the consequences of inner division and discord: *a divided heart lacks praise.* You will note that only after David has prayed, "Unite my heart," does he say, "I will praise thee, O Lord my God, with all my heart." The first is necessary to the second. Lack the one and you fail of the other. Light, strength and joy — all three of these are missing where the empire of ourselves is under a divided dominion.

Listen, soul: if you want your lips to sing, you must let the discordant thing go. If you can honestly say, "Christ is all and in all" to me, your days, whatever their shadows or their chills, will "flow in endless praise." The hymn "My Jesus, as Thou Wilt," was written years ago by a German minister, a Pastor Schmolke, who composed it as an offering of holy adoration in the midst of the most desolate circumstances. A fire had got out of control and swept over most of his parish, destroying his church and the homes of nearly all his people. A little later death took away his wife and his daughter. Then paralysis struck him and he was laid upon a bed of immovable quiet. In this condition his eyesight began to fail him. Yet there, his parish devoured by flames, blindness creeping into his eyes, bereft of wife and daughter, held fast to bed of pain, he wrote:

"My Jesus, as Thou wilt,
  Oh, let Thy will be mine;
Into Thy hand of love
  My all I now resign.
Through sorrow or through joy,
  Conduct me as Thine own,
And help me still to say,
  My Lord, Thy will be done.

My Jesus, as Thou wilt,
  Though seen through many a tear,
Let not my star of hope
  Grow dim or disappear.
Since Thou so oft hast wept
  And sorrowed all alone,
If I must weep with Thee,
  My Lord, Thy will be done.

My Jesus, as Thou wilt,
  All shall be well with me;
Each changing future scene
  I gladly trust to Thee.
Straight to my home above,
  I calmly travel on;
And say in life and death
  My Lord, Thy will be done."

III.

Surely this is the place to deal with yet another consideration: the Cure for a Divided Heart.

Do you want an end to be put to the strife within your soul? Do you really long for release from this confusion of mixed motives, and double purposes and crossed-up desires? Do you crave a unified command over the empire of your personality? If so, there are steps to be taken, and you will want to know what they are.

1. *Confess your condition.* You are well started when you stop evading the facts of your inner life and begin to call a spade a spade. "The most courageous hour in any man's life is the hour in which he honestly faces himself." The clash has been there, deep within your soul — now admit it frankly and humbly. Your eye has not been single. You have looked God's way, yes; but always there has been that side-glance toward self. Heart purity, says Kierkegard, is "to will one thing." You have willed to go along with God's will when it has been not too inconvenient. At other times you have gone your own way. Now confess it: get the whole unhappy mess out in the open light of complete honesty.

2. *Call on the Lord.* That is what David did. The text is a prayer. "Unite my heart to fear thy name." Perrowne gives a free translation of it: "Suffer my heart no longer to scatter itself upon a multiplicity of objects, to be drawn hither and thither by a thousand different aims; but turn all its powers, all its affections, in one direction, collect them in one focus, make them all one in Thee."

Scholars tell us that the Hebrew word for "unite" means to "make one." Its root is a word which means one, yet never does it mean one alone, but always a composite unit. In other words it is a blending, a coming together, a fusion.

Here is truth in the grand manner if we will grasp it. The only real blending of which the human soul is capable is the blending with God. We were made for harmony and communion with Him. The Lord Jesus became our crucified Saviour in order that He might restore in us the lost harmony with God. We have tried, many of us to find harmony in a partial salvation, an incomplete sanctification. We have identified ourselves, fitfully and feverishly, first with this

101

mood or aim and then the other. We have identified our-selves, for instance, with resentment and we've found that we weren't made for resentments: we were made for love. Resentments upset and poison us. They don't agree with us — literally, they don't. Now is the time for us to turn and say to our wounded but ever willing Lord, "Master, Thou art the only One with whom I can identify myself, the only One to whom I can give myself without reserve, and find thereby the harmony, the peace, the victory, the release for which I long."

3. *Commit yourself to God and His Word.* Our faith needs an anchor. It is therefore a helpful thing to search the Word of God for a promise and ask the Holy Spirit to seal it to you as coverage for *your* case. For example: I John 1:7 — "The blood of Jesus Christ His Son cleanseth us from all sin." Not "sins," as it is so often misquoted, but "sin." The sin of your heart, the mind of self, the root of bitterness!

Or perhaps Romans 6:11, "Reckon ye also yourselves to be dead indeed unto sin, but alive unto God through Jesus Christ our Lord." Dead indeed! No make-believe now! It is a definite, decisive, victorious stepping out of an old bondage into a new freedom. It is the declaration of a faith which claims — and receives — a *whole* Christ for the *whole* man — body, soul, and spirit—for the *whole* of life!

X.

Prayer That Prevails

~~~~~~

Text: *"Lord, teach us to pray."*—LUKE 11:1.

ONE of the queerest things about this queer age
is that so many people look upon prayer as something strange
and useless — a kind of harmless relic from the horse-and-
buggy days. It is part of a trend, and as pathetic as anything
in the general mass of absurdities and futilities in which our
age is floundering.

We have grown a generation of men and women who are
so stubbornly proud and so childishly self-conscious that
any mention of spiritual considerations outside of church is
likely to produce an awkward and embarrassing silence.
We have almost reached the place, as one minister remarked,
where the only person in the community "who can talk
about God without causing something of a sensation is the
preacher." If, for example, the chairman of a board of directors in a downtown corporation office should open the meeting by saying, "Let us pray for God's help and guidance,"
some of the directors would be stunned speechless and the
rest would begin to wonder if the business was headed for
the rocks. Yes, it makes modern folks blush to be caught
at prayers.

But why should it? Have modern folks combed all the
mystery out of life and the universe? Have they mastered
themselves, or their social chaos, or the forces of nature? Have

they the slightest reason to believe, looking at the whole problem sanely, that any one of us can stand on his own feet, independently and alone? The answer to each of these questions is a thundering negative.

In every event of our lives we are the subjects of influences that we neither originated nor can completely control. The light by which we see comes from a remote corner of the solar system. We spill a tumbler of water and it affects the farthest star. We drop a little bomb charged with the energy of a tiny uranium atom, and leave the world aghast at the threat of destroying the physical equilibrium of an entire planet. Forget the Bible for a few seconds. Just stop chattering your silly drivel about not needing any God long enough to take a correct reading of science. Even the scientists will tell you that nothing is ordinary: everything has mysterious and universal meanings. If these facts loom up with respect to the so-called physical order, how can they reasonably be denied in the realm of the spirit?

So far from denying them, one feels that he must say "Amen" to the sentiment expressed in the title of an article that recently appeared in one of our religious periodicals. "Man Must Pray or Die" is the way it read. It opened with an arresting quotation from a young woman who had been awakened to the life of prayer by a fresh study of the ministry and teaching of Jesus. Said she:

> *"Now the frontiers are all closed.*
> *Prayer is no longer a theme for eloquence,*
> *or a way of life for a few to choose*
> *whose hearts can desire it.*
> *It is the sternest necessity; the unequivocal*
> *ultimatum.*
> *There is no country we can flee to.*
> *There is no man on earth who must not face this*
> *task now."*

So, let's face it — with Jesus! Let us say, with those eager disciples of long ago, "Lord, teach us to pray."

At least two things are bound up in this request. First there is the *will* to pray. Often we misquote this passage. We make the disciples say, "Lord, teach us how to pray." The *how* is implied, no doubt, but it is not the stated thing. First comes the *will* to pray and then comes the *way* to pray. As someone has put it, the first concerns the *heart* of prayer; the second concerns the *art* of prayer.

I.

The will to pray! Let's meditate on that for a moment. Do you really want to be a man or woman of prayer? Don't be too quick to answer. It's tricky going along this path, and plenty of us are confused.

Everybody wants the things that prayer is supposed to bring, but how many of us are prepared to pay the price? How many of us realize that sometimes prayer is the mightiest when it doesn't bring us a jot or a tittle in the realm of *things?* It just brings us God!

The will to pray! How can it be aroused and fostered? By *attraction*, for one thing. This is the ideal way. It is the way that the Master used with His disciples. Many a time, in reading the verse from which our text is taken, I have lingered over the significance of the sequence which Luke describes: "And it came to pass, that, as he was praying in a certain place, *when he ceased*, one of his disciples said unto him, Lord, teach us to pray." Note the connection between His example and their exclamation. As they "listened in" on His conversation with the Father, they wondered if they had ever really known what prayer is.

Besides, it is a conviction of mine that this incident did not stand alone in their thinking. They had been watching Him for months. With Him prayer was so natural, so habitual, so unhurried, so indispensable — why were they not committed to it as He was? In Mark 1:35, for example, we read, "And in the morning, rising up a great while before day, he went out, and departed into a solitary place, and there prayed." If the scholars are right in saying that Mark received from Peter much of his material for the second Gospel, then I can guess what impressions were made upon the hearts of those apostles by the prayer habits of their Master.

Christ did not *drive* them to prayer: He *drew* them. He did not lash them: He lured them. By the sheer power of attraction He created within them an ever-mounting urge to pray.

Then life has an opposite way of stimulating the will to pray. When attraction will not serve the purpose, *affliction* takes over. The longest chapter in the Bible — Psalm 119 — is not great because of its lengthiness; it is great because of the loftiness of its insights and its instructions. In verses 67 and 71 we read: "Before I was afflicted, I went astray; but now have I kept thy Word...It is good for me that I have been afflicted; that I might learn thy statutes." God would charm us into His arms if He could; but, that failing, He must chastise us. For He knows that only in Him do we find our completion and our satisfaction.

Six months before Germany marched on Poland, an American pastor sat in seclusion with a Jewish family in the city of Berlin. The blinds were drawn. The conversation was hushed. "What has persecution done to your people?" asked the pastor. He knew that a brother-in-law had been in a concentration camp for six months. The shop which the family owned and operated had been looted and then closed. The synagogue they attended had been burned, with only its bare blackened walls remaining.

"What has persecution done to us?" replied the mother. "Many of our people had forgotten God. We, too, have our Red Sea to cross, but *we must return to the God of our fathers.*"

106

There you have it: the will to pray — to pray humbly and penitently — produced by the prod of affliction.

However it comes, whether by attraction or affliction, the important thing is that it *comes* — this dominant, driving, undiscourageable purpose to get on with the business of prayer and to have its enablements and enrichments in our lives, as others do in theirs. Hear this from a Christian leader who knows our country from North to South and from East to West: "If I were to put my finger on the greatest lack in American Christianity, I would unhesitatingly point to the need for an effective prayer life among laity and ministers."

Then let us take our stand, in weakness but in confidence, beside the apostles, saying as we do so, "Lord, teach us to *pray!*"

II.

The next thing in order is: *The way to pray!* Having charmed and challenged these men with regard to the power and possibilities of prayer, our Lord now gave them something in the way of a chart for praying. He instructed them.

He began by saying that our *approach* to prayer must be that of conscious spiritual sonship: "When ye pray, say, Our Father, which art in heaven." Perhaps you say, "Oh, well, anybody can pray." You are quite wrong. To be sure, anybody can speak words and strike poses, and call it prayer. That, however, is not what we mean by the life of communion with God.

Prayer, so Jesus taught, is conversing with God in all the intimate freedom and confident friendliness of a family conversation. In brief, prayer is friendship. How can you make a go of it, then, if you are not in the family, if you are not on friendly terms with God? There is, I grant, a sense in which the Holy Scriptures present God as having a father's heart of love toward all men — the foolish, swinish prodigal, and the proud, censorious, stay-at-home elder brother as well.

But, as Dr. J. D. Jones points out in his study of the Lord's Prayer, "though God is the Father of all men, all men are not sons." He goes on to show, with Scriptural accuracy, that, while all men are "possible sons," their "sonship becomes actual and real only in Jesus Christ."

"God," cries the apostle Paul in Galatians 4:6, "God hath sent forth the Spirit of His Son in your hearts, crying, Abba, Father." Has anything like *that* come to you? Have you taken Him at His word, that if you will commit yourself in trust to Jesus Christ His Son, He will breathe into you His very life? Have you consciously reached out to take His forgiveness, which has on it the seal of holy Blood, that thereby you may enter into a free and unhindered fellowship with Him? Frankly, do you *know* Him as Father?

It is the consciousness of this relationship which becomes the friendly, welcoming portal through which we pass into the life of prayer. Perhaps you have read the story of the little fellow who, centuries ago in Rome, broke through the ranks of soldiers and darted toward the chariot of the Emperor, who was returning from a trip abroad. Several of the guards tried to stop him, saying, "It is the Emperor!" "Yes," said the lad, "*your* emperor, but *my* father!" And a moment later he was riding where he had a right to ride - in the triumphal car with his royal father.

So some would say to us, What right have you to lift your prayer to the Infinite Majesty that presides over the universe? To which the simplest answer is, We have the right that Jesus gave us when He told us what God would be to us. The great Creator? Yes, but more. The maker of worlds? Yes, but more. The King of kings? Yes, but more. He is—"Our Father!" If you and I want to know the way of prayer, we must begin, says Jesus, with this approach.

As a further step, our Lord says something to us about the *aim* of prayer. It must have largeness of purpose. It must neither begin nor end with ourselves. It must focus in motive upon the will and glory of God. This, certainly, is the conclusion to which we are driven as we ponder the next three clauses of the model petition which Christ gave to us: "Hallowed be thy name. Thy kingdom come. Thy will be done, as in heaven, so on earth."

Plainly our triple aim in prayer must be: *the hallowing of His name, the coming of His kingdom, the doing of His will.* Some people seem to think of prayer as a kind of short-cut to having their own way. Such a false purpose will result in futile praying. Are you trying to bend God to your purposes? That is not prayer. You will know the meaning and the might of prayer when you let God bend you to His purposes and then work in you and through you to achieve those purposes.

Someone, in a happy illustration, has likened true prayer to what happens when you are in a small boat on the lake, and, coming to land, you throw out a boathook to catch hold of the shore. What happens when you pull on that boathook? You do not pull the shore to yourself, but you do pull yourself to the shore. It's the shoreline that determines where you will step out. So it is with prayer and the Divine Will. "Nevertheless," said the world's greatest Master of prayer, "not my will, but Thine be done."

Again, in showing us the way of prayer our Lord had something to say about the *attitude* of humble dependence which enables God to work through us. It is in this clause, "Give us this day our daily bread." One of the worst illusions of our times is the proud feeling of independence that has taken possession of modern man. The sooner we have this idol smashed the better it will be for all of us.

We are *not* independent. As among ourselves — individuals, communities, states, nations — we are interdependent. We cannot get along without each other. As to our relationship with God we are simply dependent — period! We can neither make our own fire or furnish our own bread. Whether you start a fire with an old-fashioned flint or a new-fashioned match, the spark comes from the sun. If there were no water power, you and I would have no electric power in our homes — and water power is nature's gift. If it were not for the seasonal kindness of sun and rain and warming earth and opening seed, how much bread would we have on our tables? It was this deeper insight which Maltbie Babcock was striving to express when he wrote:

> "Back of the loaf is the snowy flour,
> And back of the flour the mill;
> And back of the mill is the wheat, and the shower,
> And the sun, and the Father's will."

In this profound sense we are all pensioners on God's bounty. Then "Why," as the old hymn has it, "why should the spirit of mortal be proud?" Alike for our physical food and for our spiritual nourishment we are dependent upon the infinite care and the providing love of our Father above. Prayer, if we are ever to get any place with it, must recognize this fact.

Still further, our Lord points out the *atmosphere* which hovers over the path of true prayer. It is the atmosphere of humility in which one confesses his need of the mercy of God and manifests his willingness to be merciful toward others. "And forgive us our sins; for we also forgive every one that is indebted to us." The first clause is variously translated: sometimes, "Forgive us our trespasses;" sometimes "Forgive us our debts." Says Dr. A. B. Simpson, in wise comment, "There may be an honest consciousness in the heart of the suppliant that there has been no wilful or known disobedience or sin, and yet there may be infinite debt, omission, and shortcomings as compared with the high standard of God's holiness and even our own ideal." Hence we are humble enough to plead — and trustful enough to receive — the divine mercy.

In this atmosphere, however, there is something else that belongs! It is the spirit of generous forgiveness toward others, as described in the words, "For we also forgive every one that is indebted to us." Here is the crucial point where many of us are failing. Our prayers do not rise because they have not the wings of love. They do not prevail because they are poisoned and perverted by resentments and unforgiving attitudes.

Let us get this straight: when we come into God's quiet, holy presence, whether alone in our room or in the house of worship, the first required thing is to relax yourself into a state of wide-open receptivity. But with some of us, the moment we start to relax in His searching and tender presence we become uncomfortably aware that there are certain points of tension within us. Somebody's name comes to mind: hardness, tenseness, resistance. Somebody's face flashes into focus: immediately, a sense of being inwardly snarled where that person is concerned...coldness...an unmelted stoniness.

Here is where Jesus was thrusting in the needle of His truth when He said, "If thou bring thy gift to the altar, and there rememberest that thy brother hath ought against thee, leave there thy gift before the altar, and go thy way; first be reconciled to thy brother, and then come and offer thy gift" (Matthew 5:23, 24). As S. D. Gordon used to say, "The shortest way to God for that man is not the way to the altar, but around by the other man's house."

A minister and his wife had a disagreement over his pastoral appointment. He wanted to take another charge; she did not. When the bishop made his decision, appointing the man to another church, she became very bitter and resentful. Each became harsh toward the other — so much so that he let her do most of the packing of their household goods, which of course only aggravated the whole affair.

111

Already her spirit had been fouled and her prayers paralyzed by this unforgiving mood. Then came other complications. She became ill. She could not draw her breath with normal ease. She was facing, she feared, the future of an invalid. In that unhappy situation a wise and faithful counselor got hold of her. She was shown that there was a definite connection between her mental and emotional disturbance on the one hand and the nerves which controlled her breathing on the other hand. Her resentments, which had already choked her spiritual life into prayerlessness, were actually choking her physical life. Whereupon, she looked her whole problem squarely in the face, surrendered her vindictiveness and unforgiveness to God, confessed her ungraciousness to her husband, became reconciled to their new place, and arose from her invalidism, released, radiant, and useful. Once more, for her, prayer became power.

And now she could say, as you and I should be able to say as we put the crown of sovereignty on the only Head that is worthy to wear it, "*Thine* is the kingdom, and the power; and the glory for ever. Amen."

"Lord"— Thou Master of prayer —"teach us to pray!"

XI.

The World's Danger

Text: *"So shall he startle many nations."*
—Isaiah 52:15 (R.V. Margin).

Isaiah, looking toward the coming of God's Messiah, sees the Christ in an aspect which too often we forget. Not everybody, says the prophet, is going to look upon him as "the One altogether lovely." There will be those who will find Him unattractive, if not terrifying, with "visage marred more than any man." To some He will be a Messiah; to others a menace. To some He will be a deliverer; to others, merely a disturber.

This darker phase of Christ's coming among men is rarely mentioned in our Christmas poetry — a pardonable oversight, to be sure, since the major note of the Nativity is joyous and enchanting. At least one writer, however, has caught the neglected truth and pointed it up sharply in the climactic line of a brief stanza. Mary E. Coleridge puts it thus:

> *"I saw a stable, low and very bare —*
> *A little child in a manger.*
> *The oxen knew Him, had Him in care,*
> *To men He was a stranger.*
> *The safety of the world was lying there,*
> *And the world's danger."*

Christ as the world's salvation and safety is, of course, our usual way of celebrating Christmas. But Christ as "the world's danger"— how seldom we think about *that!* Let all

113

of the exquisite tenderness associated with the Christ-child be retained. We need it. We can't get on without it. At the same time let us not get quietly drunk on the soft sentiments that gather around the Holy Nativity. Remember that Baby grew up! He proved to be the God-Man, the "strong Son of God, Immortal Love," of whom Tennyson long afterward sang. Although He never lost His tenderness, He impressed many men not as the Tender One but as the Terrible One. He became Jesus the disturber. Isaiah proved to be right: He was the *startling* Christ! He was "the world's danger."

I.

For one thing, Jesus Christ has always been a danger to *closed and prejudiced minds.* Someone has well said that "There is no pain like the pain of a new idea." The tendency of the adult mind is to go stale. We furnish a snug little thought-world with certain ideas and opinions, and then steadfastly resist the very suggestion that we might profitably add a piece or two of furniture or even a whole new room!

It was the closed mind that by-passed the modest town of Bethlehem, never dreaming that the Son of God might choose so unlikely a spot as His birthplace. Yet Jesus took humble Bethlehem and made it the Christmas capital of the world. To be sure, the prophet had foretold it all, but the small minds of the worldly-wise have no room for a prophet's message: "thou, Bethlehem Ephratah, though thou be little among the thousands of Judah, yet out of thee shall he come forth unto me that is to be ruler in Israel" (Micah 5:2).

It was the closed mind that asked in oft-repeated proverb, "Can any good thing come out of Nazareth?" Yet the holiest Being that ever graced this often graceless planet spent thirty years of His life in that despised community, thereby hallowing for all time the very sound of its name.

It was the closed mind that listened to the teachings of Jesus and then exclaimed, in bewilderment and derision, "How knoweth this man letters, having never learned?" (John 7:15). Or, as we might say, "What college has He attended, that He should presume to teach us?" Yet Jesus, Who was never graduated from any school of rabbis or priests, has been the inspiration for the founding of more colleges and seminaries and the writing of more books than any teacher of all time. Such is the irony of history! Such is the danger of the Galilean to the petty prejudices of frozen minds!

It was the closed mind that sent back its quick and resentful rejoinder, "How is it that thou, being a Jew, askest drink of me who am a woman of Samaria?" Jesus took that expression of racial pride and religious exclusiveness and, casting it forever aside, declared that true worth and true worship were not matters of skin and caste but rather of spirit and attitude: "God is a spirit, and they that worship him must worship him in spirit and in truth" (John 4:24).

Make no mistake about it, our small and ungracious prejudices are never safe with the manger-cradled Christ around. They are condemned. They are always uneasy. In the end, they must be broken up and altogether banished. One night in 1924, when feeling against France and the Negro was running high in Germany because colored French troops were patrolling the Rhineland, that fine Negro tenor, Roland Hayes, stood on a concert stage in Berlin, ready to sing the opening number of a scheduled program. But the audience blasted him with its hisses. Hayes stood there, in the curve of the grand piano, just "taking it." His eyes were closed and in his heart was a prayer — a prayer of Christian love and good will.

Ten minutes later, when the hissing and the stamping of feet had ceased, Hayes signalled to his accompanist for a switch in number. Softly, almost in a whisper, he began

115

to sing Schubert's "Thou Art My Peace." As the clear tenor notes floated out over the crowd a complete silence prevailed. At the end of the hour, even after two French numbers had been rendered, deafening applause broke loose. While it continued, part of the crowd surged up onto the stage, lifted Roland Hayes onto its shoulders and carried the black singer off in a delirium of admiration.

"It was not a personal victory," said Hayes, "it was the victory of a Force that sang through me and won that audience. It was allowing myself to be used by a Power that is greater than I am, and it subdued the hatred of that audience."

You and I know what that "Power" is of whom the singer speaks. It is the power of this dangerous Christ, who will have no truck with our senseless prejudices of race and religion, who is set instead for the triumph of humility over arrogance and of understanding over bigotry.

II.

Let us be reminded, in the second place, that our Lord Jesus Christ has always been a danger to *selfish and exploiting interests*. Few things about the teachings He expounded are more startling to the nations of this world than His stand on greed and exploitation. He declared, "Whosoever will save his life shall lose it: and whosoever will lose his life for my sake shall find it. For what is a man profited if he shall gain the whole world, and lose his own soul?" (Matthew 16:25, 26). That was enough to stamp Him as a radical and a revolutionary.

Radical it may be, but after two thousand years psychologists are recognizing the truth of it as applied both to personal and social living.

Was it not *dangerous* for that Rich Young Ruler to come to the Master? Did he find Jesus a "soft-soaper," ready to hand him some inocuous package that might be described as an opiate? Anything but that! What Christ said to him was dynamite: "Go and sell that thou hast, and give to the poor . . . and come and follow me" (Matthew 19:21).

Was it not *dangerous* for those scribes and Pharisees to expose themselves to Jesus' withering blasts about the avarice that hides beneath the cloak of religion? "You love to make long prayers," said He, "standing in the market place while you do it; but you also love to devour widows' houses. . . How can you escape the damnation of hell?" (Matthew 23:14).

Was it not *dangerous* for two of His own disciples and their mother to come with the request that they be given preferred positions of honor, one on the right hand and the other on the left, in the coming Kingdom? Jesus put them in their place by assuring them that honors in the Kingdom were not passed out by whim, as politicians pass out their plums and plaudits. With crushing solemnity the Master asked, "Are ye able to be baptized with my baptism?" Seek great things for yourself, and they will elude your grasp forever. Seek the glory of God, and all worthy greatness will come to you.

Christ is still the menace of this world's greed — your greed, or mine, or anyone's else. Listen to this: "A case was discovered. . . in which thirty-four female slaves were crammed for sleeping quarters into a hole in a ship 'measuring only 9 feet 4 inches in length, 4 feet 8 inches main breadth, and 2 feet 7 inches in height.'" Sounds like a flash report from some German or Japanese atrocity experiment as of 1945, doesn't it? Well, that was the condition of things on one of the 136 British ships which, during the year before the Revolutionary War, were engaged exclusively in the traffic in human slavery. At the base of the whole infamous business, in England as later in the United States, was the lust for profits. And when vested interests get their steel fingers around something that they can exploit for huge financial gain, no matter what it is — stock markets, horse racing, prostitution, liquor or slavery — you may be sure that their hold will be hard to break.

What happened to legalized slavery in Britain? Some preachers, be it admitted, tried to defend it. Lawyers built up strong cases for its perpetuation. There was just one thing that doomed it: Christ was against it. He was its challenge, its menace and its ruin. William Wilberforce was His voice in the British Parliament and John Wesley in the forum of popular address. Wesley did not live to see the victory. Six days before his death he wrote a letter to Wilberforce:

"Unless God has raised you up for this very thing," he said, "you will be worn out by the opposition of men and devils; but if God be for you, who can be against you? Are all of them together stronger than God? Oh, be not weary in well doing. Go on, in the name of God and in the power of His might, till even American slavery, the vilest that ever saw the sun, shall vanish away before it."

A quarter of a century later, as Wilberforce lay dying, messengers from Westminster entered his room to tell him that at last the Emancipation Bill had been passed. "Thank God!" exclaimed the dying man, "thank God! I've lived to see this day."

Ah, man, put your finger on any cancerous thing you can find in human life or society, anything that fattens on the weakness, ignorance or defenselessness of human beings. It may flourish for awhile. It may wax hellishly brazen for a time. But it's never safe with Jesus Christ loose in the world. He is always its danger; He will ultimately be its doom.

III.

Again, Jesus has always been dangerous to *casual and formal professors of religion*. He startled men by the quiet ruthlessness with which He tore the cloak of pride and unreality from their shallow piety.

He made them gulp and blink as He said to them, "Take heed that ye do not your alms before men, to be seen of them. otherwise ye have no reward of your Father which is in heaven" (Matthew 6:1). With Christ looking on, its dangerous to be religiously insincere.

He made them wince as He said, "When ye stand praying, forgive if ye have ought against any, that your heavenly Father also may forgive you your trespasses" (Mark 11:25). With Christ's eye upon you, it is dangerous to attempt the mild blasphemy of praying to God in a display of piety when you are relentless and unforgiving toward any person in the world.

He made them turn pale as He pictured the self-satisfied and superior air of the Pharisee who, looking with disdain upon a publican, prayed, "God, I thank thee that I am not as other men." With Christ in the offing, a hard self-righteousness, devoid of humility and compassion, is never safe! Never!

How much of reality and consistency does the Lord see in us? His eyes are as a flame of fire, we read, and they are searching us. Too many of us, it may be, are Christmas-tree Christians — all decorated and tinselled today, and tomorrow lying prone and stripped among the rubbish. We are "prettied up" with prayers and hymns on Sunday and bedraggled like the rest of the world during the week.

A committeewoman of a national organization — an organization that carries the word "Christian" in its title — was getting ready to attend a conference. "I must go a day ahead," said she, "so I can get my drinking over before the

119

conference begins." She did, and in doing so she dragged down a young woman who had been struggling with drink. All the clever "rationalizations" in the world can never bring Christ over on the side of that sort of thing.

It was a church member who said, with a giggle of unconcealed delight, "I took the hymn number on Sunday morning and won fifty dollars on it." There's a wedding for you: the form of godliness married to the fashion of gambling!

Now upon all this tragic mockery of real religious devotion our Lord looks with a discerning and dangerous eye. He sees it for what it is: an empty profession, a heartless formality. He will have none of it, as He openly declares that harlots and publicans will go into the Kingdom ahead of church members and creed-mongers.

IV.

And then, once more, Jesus has always been a danger to *evil-doers who either defy the moral order of God or else despair of being harmonized with it.*

Take the case of Herod the king. He was terrified when he heard tidings of Jesus' birth. He sought cruelly and remorselessly to destroy Him. Was Herod a fool to entertain such a fear? By no means. It was a sound, even though misdirected, instinct within his evil heart that made him fear Jesus. That defenseless Babe, lying there in the manger, was in fact a terrifying threat to everything in life that Herod represented: its lust and licentiousness, its contempt for the weak and the helpless, its gross and showy materialism, its mailed fist of unscrupulous violence. Of course this Christ of God was a menace — a terrific and implacable menace — to that whole rotten way of living. Today Herod's name

awakens nothing but disgust while of Jesus we sing in wor-
shipful adoration:

> *"All hail the power of Jesus' name,*
> *Let angels prostrate fall;*
> *Bring forth the royal diadem,*
> *And crown Him Lord of all."*

Bring the story up to date if you will. Some time ago,
even before Hitler had met his fate, Wm. C. Kernan, Director
of the Christian Institute for American Democracy, wrote:
"It has taken ten years since the rise of Hitler to make us
see that men who renounce sound moral principles have only
the alternative left of acting like animals in response to the
demands of their unbridled passions and instincts." And
what is the outcome, one may ask? What has happened to
Hitler and the arrogant horde of Nazi leaders who, from
the same motives that prompted Herod of old, sought to
banish the gentle Jesus born of a Jewish virgin? They, too,
realized that Jesus was a threat to their insane plans. Where
are they now? Defeated, discredited, disgraced, and either
dead or doomed to die! What was said about the enemies
of the infant Jesus may now be said of these modern foes of
the Galilean: "They are dead which sought the young child's
life!" He is still the world's danger!

The note, however, on which to end this message must
be much more personal. Not many of us openly defy the
moral ideal which God has revealed in His Son. With
most of us the guilt we bear lies along a line that is much
more subtle. We have tried to reconcile ourselves to an easy-
going existence that has in it not too much of evil and
not too seriously much of good. We shrug off our sins by
saying, "Oh, well, that's just human nature." We justify
our devilish disposition by the remark, "My peculiar tem-
perament, you know; I got it from my grandfather." We
close our eyes to the blinding white light of a really Christ-

like life, telling ourselves as we do so that "It's just a fanciful and impossible ideal anyhow."

Yet all the while we are strangely uncomfortable. All the while the "Hound of Heaven" is after us. All the while this holy, redeeming Christ is disturbing us, convicting us, endangering the smug, specious comfort into which we have tried to settle ourselves. Let Dorothy Sayers interpret it for us:

> *"Thou liest, Christ, Thou liest; take it hence,*
> *That mirror of strange glories; I am I;*
> *What wouldest Thou make of me? O cruel pretence*
> *Drive me not mad so with the mockery*
> *Of that most lovely, unattainable lie!*

No, that is not irreverence. That is the poetic effort to say that Jesus Christ *does* give us an example that is too high for us to follow. And when we, thinking to excuse ourselves because the ideal is so unattainable by any poor effort of ours, settle back to our poor and shabby way of living, He will not let us rest.

"I offer you more than my example," says He. "I offer you *Myself*. Let me come in to be at home in your heart. Let Me speak the healing word of forgiveness and peace to your condemned soul. Let Me release My power in your impotent being. Let Me be your Saviour!"

What do you say to that? On your answer — an answer He is asking for in this very hour — hangs the determination of what Jesus Christ will be to you: your danger or your deliverer, your ruin or your redemption!

XII.

When Responsibility Closes In

TEXT: *"So then every one of us shall give account of himself to God."*—ROMANS 14:12.

As in our day so in Paul's day, it was so much easier to sit in judgment on other people than to sit in judgment on ourselves. Furthermore, it has always been fatally easy for us to forget that each of us and all of us must eventually stand or fall before a higher tribunal than man's. "All of us," reads the Moffatt New Testament, "have to stand before the tribunal of God... Each of us then will have to answer for himself to God."

This closing in of responsibility to the point where it becomes urgently and inescapably personal is a note that needs to be struck again in our day. Actually the "forgotten man" in today's world is not this man or that, representing some social or economic group; the "forgotten man" is just the "forgotten *man*." "Men"—oh, yes, that's different. Men in the mass, making up the pawns that are to be moved around by the all-powerful state on the chessboard of political manipulation! Men in the mass, making up the human cogs in the intricate and largely soulless economic machine! Men in the mass, making up the impersonal units — platoons, companies, regiments, divisions — of personality-crushing armies! We have had no end of this sort of thing. And that's just the mischief of it.

As a result there has been, during the last two generations, a progressive fading out of the sense of individual responsibility. If I fail, society is to blame. If there is help to be given let the government give it. So the feeling has grown that personal accountability does not count for much.

I.

First of all, then, let us see more particularly what it is that explains our *evasions* of individual responsibility in the important concerns of life.

For one thing, a good deal that has called itself modern education has been at fault. Go back a few years, and you have science teaching men that the universe is a mindless machine in which such spiritual factors as the soul, or sin, or free will, or even God, simply do not exist outside of the imagination of the pious. It was the day of the scientific doctrine of determinism. It meant, in effect, that freedom is an illusion and fate is all. Where is personal responsibility in a world system such as that?

Go back a few years, and you have psychology teaching our young people that human behavior has nothing to do with so-called principles or concepts. Man's behavior is essentially an animal response to animal stimuli, since man, after all, is only an animal with a somewhat more sensitive organism than the animals beneath him. Therefore, said this school of psychology, what you want to do is right; what you do not want to do is wrong. Men are not bad because they have bad hearts; they are bad (or rather unfortunate) because they have bad glands.

In my college days that was the one-tenth of truth that was dished out for the whole truth. The manner in which it was done, however, made it sheer moral poison for those who fell for it. Those were the days when Ogden Nash might have been crowned the poet laureate of this half-baked philosophy of life. Nash wrote the couplet:

*"Why did the Lord give us agility.
If not to escape responsibility?"*

It would be hard to find two lines that look with more leering eyes upon all the sacred things of life. It reflects the mood of the very modern individual who, when told by a friend that he was acting like a fool, came back with the shoulder-shrugging reply, "Well, if that is what I am, I cannot help it. That is the way fate made me."

Another thing that has contributed to the current breakdown of the sense of personal responsibility is the development, in one degree or another, of state socialism. The extreme illustration of it was to be found, of course, in the Nazi Germany of the late Adolph Hitler. Two or three years before the outbreak of the war individual freedom had been so effectively crushed in the Third Reich that Hermann Goering was able to announce publicly: "The private person is no longer wanted in Germany." Bluntly, the state is all; the individual as such is nothing. What that kind of government does in time to the consciousness of personal freedom and accountability is obvious enough. Men knuckle under, like the industrialists, the professors and many of the pastors of Germany did, or they stand out against it and go to prison, as Martin Niemoller did.

In our own country, as we all know, there has been a wider and wider extension of what we may call public services or socialized responsibility. It has come necessarily. So much of it has been good. Yet, for all that, most thoughtful people will tell you that it has had a tendency to destroy our realization of personal responsibility. Want a job? Let the government guarantee you one. Want to build a home? Let the government make you a loan. Want medical and hospital services? Let the government provide them. Want

125

sickness and old age security? Let the government furnish it. And on we go.

This is no attempt to argue the point of governmental control one way or the other. It is only a way of pointing out to all of us that the farther we go on the side of collectivism and state socialism the more difficult it is to keep alive a wholesome sense of private responsibility for life, for duty and for destiny.

Or again, one is bound to say that there are those who shirk individual responsibility by falling into the snare of self-pity. They waste perfectly good time feeling sorry for themselves either because of their bad ancestry or their ugly environment. No sane person denies the influence of heredity, but a lot of people have talked insanely about some fancied hereditary handicap of theirs. A young person said, "I don't like classical music, but why should I? My father and my grandfather never did." We're often just about as shallow as that when we talk about heredity.

So, too, with circumstances — we can cry over them or we can climb over them. The choice is up to us. An elderly man recently said to a young minister, "I'm thankful I'm not as young as you are; I should hate to live much longer in this kind of a world." There's something pathetic about that. The evil of the world is admittedly tragic. Yet the whole mass of its evil is not great enough or powerful enough to crush or contaminate one single soul that flings itself boldly and believingly on God and forges ahead.

Responsible living — that's what these times demand. That's what God has always asked of us. And that, let it be added, is what He is going to ask of us when we stand before Him to be judged. It is not living that we need to fear. What we need to beware of is the effort, conscious or unconscious, to shrug off our personal responsibility for taking this thing called living and, in allegiance to Jesus Christ, doing something fine with it.

II.

Consider, in the next place, some of the *expressions* of this law of personal responsibility in Christian living.

From the point of view of our text and its relation to the context, the first fact we face is that *each of us is responsible for a cultivated conscience*. It is the adjective that is important: the Christian *cultivation* of the conscience is what Paul wanted these early Christians to know. One man was asked if he had a "good conscience." His cynical reply was: "I should say so — as good as new; it has never been used." It was only a quip, perhaps, and intended as a half-truth, but it points up a serious phase of our living: conscience as such is not to be trusted; it must be an informed and healthy conscience.

See now how the Apostle Paul deals with this question. In the Christian community in Rome, as in others among Paul's churches, there were those who had been converted to Christ out of paganism and those who had been converted to Christ out of Judaism. Those of Hebrew background and training were accustomed to an elaborate system of regulations and restrictions that went far beyond the Ten Commandments. This was particularly true if they had belonged to one of the stricter sects, such as the Pharisees or the Essenes. The more extreme among them would feel, for example, that if they let a new moon pass as an ordinary day, the Lord's favor would be withdrawn from them.

In the other group were these Christians with a pagan background. For them no such ceremonial scruples ever existed. For their salvation they placed no dependence whatever upon such observances of form and ritual. They were trusting in Christ alone and were concentrating on the fundamental moral and spiritual duties which went along with loyalty to Christ. They had no feeling that eating meat, even meat that had been used in connection with heathen rituals, would contaminate their souls.

Since their brethren in the other camp felt otherwise, there developed this clash and friction which threatened the well-being of the church as a whole. The solution which Paul proposed was a more enlightened conscience on both sides. The enlightenment was to take two forms: a recognition of the Christian principle of *liberty* and a recognition of the Christian principle of *responsibility*.

What about the liberty? Look at verse five: "Let every man be persuaded in his own mind." There you have it. But in fairness to Paul you want to be clear as to the sort of liberty he is commending. This is the same Paul who writes to the Galatian Christians, saying, "Though we, or an angel from heaven preach any other gospel unto you, . . . let him be accursed" (Galatians 1:8). Why does he not say to the Galatians, "Let every man be fully persuaded in his own mind"? Because there he is discussing something entirely different. There it is a question of Christ as the Son of God and the Cross of Christ as the essential way of salvation. A man has no liberty to deny *that*, cries the Apostle, and call himself a Christian.

But here in the Roman church the problems that are vexing and straining the brotherhood have nothing to do with basic doctrines of the faith or fundamental Christian morals. They are rather the external questions of form and custom. This calls for the exercise of Christian liberty by both parties.

Ah, that is fine, you say. That's the kind of conscience I believe in — one that is elastic on these secondary matters. Very well, says Paul, but combined with this principle of liberty is the sense of responsibility. You've got to build *that* into your conscience, too.

God will hold you responsible for a harsh and condemning criticism of those you call narrow. After all, says Paul, "to him that esteemeth anything to be unclean, to him it is unclean" (v. 14). To bring it down to date, if he feels that smoking, for example, is unclean, while you feel that it is not, you are to hold him, not in contempt, but in respect.

On the other hand, he is under the same obligation toward you, assuming, of course, that there are the *essential* evidences of your faith in Christ and your devotedness to Him. He is not to judge you unworthy of a place in Christ's Church *merely* because of a difference of this kind.

Splendid, says someone, that should end the matter. Oh, no, says Paul. It does not end the matter at all. The principle of responsibility holds on us a still tighter rein. The enlightened Christian conscience, he now shows, must include a concern for the influence that my broader views and practices may have upon others in the brotherhood of the church. In other words, there are *limits* on my Christian liberty which I voluntarily accept for the sake of others. And here is Paul's way of stating it: "Let us not therefore judge one another any more" (this is our liberty); "but judge this rather, that no man put a stumbling-block or an occasion to fall in his brother's way" (this is the limitation that we are willing — and obligated — to place on our liberty). "Make up your mind never to put any stumbling-block or hindrance in your brother's way," is the simpler, terser form in which Moffatt renders it.

It often looks as if we Christians of today, in our emphasis upon being broad and exercising freedom, have forgotten that part of our responsibility. We have neglected that element in the training and sensitizing of our Christian conscience. Take *that* into account, my friends, and see what it does to your practice of smoking, your so-called moderate drinking, your theater-going, your card-playing, your careless observance of the Lord's Day, and the like. It is so much easier, you see, to plead for liberty than it is to shoulder responsibility.

If it be objected that now the preacher has come down to the level of negative talk and trifling issues, then he can only answer that St. Paul made the same descent when he wrote the Epistle to the Romans. When these matters need to be handled, as they sometimes do, then certainly we should know what Christian principles are involved. Clearly we should be more interested in a cultivated than a callous conscience. For in the end "every one of us shall give account of himself to God."

We pass now to think about another direction in which this truth of personal accountability expresses itself. It is just this: *each of us is personally responsible for a careful and constructive use of his opportunities.* Listen again to the Holy Spirit speaking through the Apostle Paul. It is a passage in II Corinthians, chapter 5, which somewhat parallels the one out of which our text is taken: "For we must all appear before Christ's judgment seat in our true light, in order that each may receive an award for his actions in this life, in accordance with what he has done, whether it be good or bad. Knowing then what the fear of the Lord means, we endeavor to win men" (II Corinthians 5:10, 11, Weymouth).

Do you realize that when we stand before the searching eyes of Jesus Christ, He is not going to ask us what church we joined, or by what mode we were baptized, or whether we accepted the Augsburg or the Westminster Confession, or a dozen other things that we often argue about? Do we realize that He *is* going to ask us, His disciples, what we did with that commission of His: "Go ye into all the world and preach the gospel to every creature"? He *is* going to ask us what we did to win our children, and our friends, and our associates to a new life in Christ. He *is* going to ask us what we did with our opportunities to challenge people with the question of their personal relationship to the Redeemer who died for them.

And what are we going to answer? We who can "talk shop" so constantly, and current events so informatively, and politics so avidly, and the weather so casually, but who are strangely silent on matters that would prick a man's spiritual indifference and set him thinking about his soul! We who say we believe that the main business of Christ's Church is to mediate the miracle of the new birth in the lives of men, but who rarely if ever, invite someone to accompany us to the place where the renewing Gospel of the grace of God will be preached! We who have money to spend for everything else, but who either pass up the offering for foreign missions or else dole out a sum so paltry that it wouldn't equal one week's spending on the movies! What, I ask you, what, in the name of that bleeding Saviour on the Cross, are we going to answer?

A professional woman entered into a transforming experience of our Lord Jesus Christ. She was a skilled lecturer on home economics, giving addresses and demonstrations that drew thousands of women to hear and see her. Shortly after her conversion she was heard by one woman who wrote her impressions to a friend: "She stopped in the midst of her three-hour cooking lecture and witnessed to eighteen hundred people, putting over the idea of women's responsibility in the home, not primarily as cooks, but as changed people. The newspaper sponsors were dumbfounded. I talked with one of them and complimented him on the fine school, and mentioned the fact that the lecturer had talked to the women about their spiritual lives. He replied, 'She talked to me about my relationship to Christ.'"

She was, as Paul would say, "buying up her opportunity." She was making ready to stand with clean hands before the "judgment seat of Christ." You never have a chance to stand before eighteen hundred people? Granted. But what about the eighteen that you *could* sit down and list, who need your witness as to what Christ has done for you?

131

Responsibility closes in. Our evasions will not do. They are hurtful to others and damaging to ourselves. For a conscience that is alive and sensitive to all the unveiled meanings of the mind of Christ — for that I am myself responsible. For a consecrated service which makes the winning of others to Christ its chief and changeless goal, and which will not knowingly pass up its opportunities for reaching this goal — for that, too, I bear a responsibility which cannot be escaped.

> "Therefore, O Lord, I will not fail nor falter,
>   Nay, but I ask it, nay, but I desire,
> Lay on my lips Thine embers of the altar,
>   Seal with the sting and furnish with the fire.
>
> Give me a voice, a cry, and a complaining —
>   Oh! let my sound be stormy in their ears!
> Throat that would shout but cannot stay for straining,
>   Eyes that would weep but cannot stay for tears.
> Quick in a moment, infinite forever,
>   Send an arousal better than I pray,
> Give me a grace upon the faint endeavor,
>   Souls for my hire and Pentecost today."

That is the flaming fashion in which F. W. H. Myers interprets the mind and passion of the prince of apostles in his profound poem, *St. Paul.* God send the flame of it into your soul and mine — we who, in these hushed moments, have faced the fact that "every one of us must give account of himself to God."

XIII.

The Dispossessed Possessors

~~~~~~

Text: *"Ye are not your own."*—I Corinthians 6:19.
"All things are yours."—I Corinthians 3:21.

THE effort to state the whole of truth often pushes us into seeming contradictions. Paul found it so. Indeed, Jesus found it so. One thinks of such a statement as, "He that loveth his life shall lose it; and he that hateth his life shall keep it unto life eternal." One thinks again of the words, "Peace I leave with you, my peace I give unto you," combined with the words, "Think not that I am come to send peace on the earth: I came not to send peace but a sword."

On the face of them these are contradictory utterances, but when they are probed to the bottom and understandingly interpreted they are found to be harmonious parts of a larger whole.

So it is with our text: "Ye are not your own . . . all things are yours." The two clauses seem to conflict with each other; and yet in point of fact they stand in closest connection, each one a hemisphere, so to speak, and both together forming one perfect sphere of truth.

The Christian, according to St. Paul, must be dispossessed of himself. This comes through his being possessed by Christ. Then he, in turn, through Christ, becomes the possessor of a wealth that actually sweeps the far reaches of the universe.

I.

"Ye are not your own." This is one side of the coin, of which the other side is revealed in the words that appear in connection with our second clause: "Ye are Christ's" or, as another translation has it, "You belong to Christ." "All things are yours," is an announcement we welcome. The more selfish and greedy we are the more it appeals to us. What we are not so keen to grasp is the profound fact that this vast wealth opens to us only as we renounce ourselves in favor of Another, and that Other is the Lord of all souls and the Lord of all things.

"Ye are not your own." It is this dispossession from which we naturally recoil. Self-willed, self-centered, self-assertive creatures that we are, we insist on belonging to ourselves. We must manage our affairs. We must carve out a grand destiny for ourselves. We must take care of Number One. And instead of really taking care of Number One, by giving it to God and enriching it with the sort of goods you cannot buy at drug stores, or super-markets, or real estate offices, we think only or chiefly of perishable values. Then we wonder why the rewards that come as we trudge the end of life's trail are so meager and disappointing. We are like the man who said bitterly, "I have worked all my life for food and clothes, and now the food doesn't agree with me and the clothes won't fit me."

There are masses of people whose experience is accurately described in the searching lines:

> "They live for themselves, they think for themselves,
>   For themselves and for none beside;
> Just as if Jesus had never lived,
>   As if He had never died."

Do you catch the significance of that line, "Just as if Jesus had never lived"? Whether you like it or not, Jesus of Nazareth has been in this world of ours, and since He has been here it just cannot be the same world. By His living He gave us a new conception of life and by His dying He put a new claim upon life. That is what Paul means when he says, "Ye are not your own. For ye are bought with a price: therefore glorify God in your body, and in your spirit, which are God's."

Even Christ "pleased not Himself." He declared that His "meat" and His "drink" were to do the will of His Father. He said He came not "to be ministered unto, but to minister." Such is the conception of life He gave us. But I beg of you, do not think of it only as a conception. It is also a claim upon life. When I watch that Man, Christ Jesus, move sinlessly across the stage of our world and then, notwithstanding His sinlessness, I see Him die for sinners like me: when I see Him meet hate with love, impurity with holiness, fear with courage, irritation with patience, malice with mercy, deceit with honesty, injustice with righteousness: then I know with some sure instinct of my soul that here life has found its Key. Here, without doubt, is the meaning of life. Here, too, is the power by which my life can be changed and remolded so as to enable me to realize that meaning.

Before we go any further with this message, then, we need to pause and raise with ourselves this very personal, pointed question: Am I my own, or do I belong to Christ? Christ belongs to me, of course, just as He belongs to the whole world of men for whom He died. He belongs to me, moreover, in the sense that I have been taught to believe in Him and to reverence Him. But do I belong to Him — honestly, utterly, enthusiastically? Do I? Does He know that I do? Does the world know that I do? Do the friends who know me best realize that I do? Does His ownership, His sovereignty, in me extend all the way down to the deeps of my soul and all the way out to the circumference of my life?

A few years ago the Salvation Army held a world-wide celebration to commemorate the one hundredth anniversary of the birth of General William Booth. I was living in Detroit, and a friend of mine there brought me a copy of the beautiful Centennial number of the *War Cry*. It was a superb piece of journalism, as befitted the memory of the man whose extraordinary career it was honoring. In one of the articles was a sentence that lingers with me to this hour: "William Booth, king among men so long as the world counts service the badge of royalty." The service was rendered, and the world has not withheld its recognition of the kingliness of the soul who rendered it. But, it may be asked, wherein lay the secret of such service as came from the heart and hand of General Booth? For answer one goes to a scene near the end of the General's life. Dr. J. Wilbur Chapman was in London. He asked for and received opportunity to interview the Army's white-haired leader. "General Booth," said he, "what would you say has been the one chief secret of your life and the blessings that have attended it?" To which the grand old man replied, "The secret is this: *I long ago resolved that God should have all there is of William Booth!*"

There you have it: dispossessed of self, possessed with Christ and, through Christ, in possession of all things.

"Ye are not your own. . . . All things are yours."

II.

Consider the wealth that is reckoned to us if we in fact belong to Christ. Paul is God's certified accountant in this matter, and he sets forth in magnificent tabulation the range and fulness of our riches: "All things are yours; whether Paul, or Apollos, or Cephas, or the world, or life, or death, or things present, or things to come; all are yours; and ye are Christ's; and Christ is God's."

1. For one thing, all true teachers and ministers of Christ are yours: "Whether Paul, or Apollos, or Cephas." There

136

was friction in the Christian community in Corinth. Personal and partisan loyalties to men had become more important than the common loyalty of all to Christ. So one said, "I belong to Paul"; another, "I belong to Apollos"; a third, "I belong to Cephas." There were "Paulites," "Apollosites," and "Cephasites." They were party-minded and sect-minded when they should have been Christ-minded.

Paul, with unerring spiritual precision, puts his finger on the trouble: "You have got out of focus," says he. "You have missed your center and when you are off at the center, you are off all around. You do not belong to Paul or to Apollos or to any other teacher. You belong to Christ, and then, with this central relationship recognized, you will find that Paul and Apollos and Cephas belong to you."

There is a lesson of immeasurable value here for the Christians of our day. Christ is the Truth. That is our basic belief as Christians. He has many witnesses, many interpreters, many teachers. But these interpreters, being finite and frail, have their limitations. Not one of them can say the last word on any line of Christian interpretation on which he may speak. The whole cargo is much too great for his tiny vessel. Even Paul, mighty as he was in intellect and spirit, could not give us all that we needed for a complete New Testament. Who can doubt the divine wisdom that selects a Peter and a John and a James to make their contribution to our New Testament revelation of Christ and His redemptive purposes through the Church?

There is a small, sectarian mind that one occasionally encounters which needs the same surgical treatment that Paul gave the Corinthians. There is, on the other hand, a mind that is open, not to anything and everything that comes down the pike, but to anything that springs from the spirit and the truth of the Master. Our hymns, perhaps better than our theologies, illustrate how rich is the contribution that has been made to our understanding and worship of Christ by

men of all nations and doctrinal backgrounds.
We all sing:

> *"All hail the power of Jesus' name,*
> *Let angels prostrate fall;*
> *Bring forth the royal diadem,*
> *And crown Him Lord of all."*

Who wrote that? Edward Peronnet, a Protestant.
But we also sing:

> *"Jesus, the very thought of Thee,*
> *With sweetness fills the breast,*
> *But sweeter far Thy face to see,*
> *And in Thy presence rest."*

Who wrote that? Bernard of Clairvaux, a Catholic.
We sing:

> *"How sweet the name of Jesus sounds*
> *In a believer's ears;*
> *It soothes his sorrows, heals his wounds,*
> *And drives away His fears."*

Who wrote that? John Newton, a ritual-loving Anglican.
But we also sing:

> *"O Lord and Master of us all,*
> *Whate'er our name or sign,*
> *We own Thy sway, we hear Thy call,*
> *We test our lives by Thine."*

And that was written by John G. Whittier, a ritual-repudi-
ating Quaker.

Here, then, is one slice of our vast fortune if we are not
our own but Christ's: all true Christ-honoring teachers belong to us. We can appropriate their treasures with grateful joy.

2. Paul's next claim is an audacious one. He says that the
"world" belongs to Christians. Perhaps this strikes us with
surprise. We have thought of Christians as having as little

to do with the world as possible, as being in fact afraid of it, opposed to it, trying always to escape from it. Yet Paul boldly declares the world is ours if only we are Christ's.

Partly, of course, it is a question of defining the meaning of our term. There is a world which men have fashioned — a world of business and politics and pleasure — from which Christ is ruled out. It is to a large extent an artificial world, a pagan world, an unworthy world. If we have the mind of Christ, frankly this world does not belong to us or we to it. But there is another world, partly of God's making and partly of man's making, which is quite different. It is a world of mountains and lakes, of flowers and birds, of summers and winters, of music and art, of culture and love. In the deepest and highest meaning of the word, no one can *possess* this world quite as truly as the Christian soul. For, mind you, ownership in this realm is not nearly so much a matter of money with which to purchase, and title deeds to which one may point with pride, as it is a matter of artistic and spiritual appreciation.

I knew a man and his wife in Michigan who for years lived in close proximity to poverty. They kept going through the generosity of a son and a few friends of theirs. They were supremely lovers of Christ and secondarily lovers of nature. Their little flower garden was a work of art. They tended it with the carefulness and tenderness of a lover. A little distance from where they lived were the mansions and estates of some of Detroit's richest men. And verily I say unto you this humble couple, with the brand-marks of Christ upon them, came far nearer owning the world of flowers and birds than most of the millionaires around them, whose legal holdings were far greater but whose appreciations were far more meager.

It is just this thing that Charles Mackey is trying to say in his striking poem called *Cleon's Possessions:*

"Cleon hath a million acres, not a one have I;
Cleon dwelleth in a palace, in a cottage I;
Cleon hath a dozen fortunes, not a penny I;
Yet the poorer of the twain is Cleon, and not I.

Cleon, true, possesses acres, but the landscape I;
Half the charm to me it yieldeth money cannot buy;
Cleon harbors sloth and dulness, freshening vigor I;
He is velvet, I in fustian, richer man am I.

Cleon is a slave to grandeur, free as thought am I;
Cleon fees a score of doctors, need of none have I;
Wealth-surrounded, care-environed, Cleon fears to die;
Death may come, he'll find me ready, happier man am I.

Cleon sees no charm in nature, in a daisy I;
Cleon hears no anthems ringing in the sea and sky;
Nature sings to me forever, earnest listener I;
State for state, with all attendants, who would change? Not I."

3. Something else belongs to the Christian, according to St. Paul. He calls it "life." Is life something to be escaped, as the Buddhists say, and indeed as many a fed-up worldling says, or is it something to be faced — and fulfilled? Paul says it is the latter. If we have taken hold of life at its center and made it ours, then we shall be able to handle whatever comes out of life at any point on the circumference. The Center is Christ, who said, "I am the way, the truth and the life." Because Life has conquered us, we can conquer life.

In recent years the question has often been raised: Do you find life worth living? My answer to that query is, No, nobody *finds* life worth living; he has to *make* life worth living. And the secret of the "making" is found adequately, joyously, achievingly, in Jesus Christ our Lord. He did not *find* life worth while; He had to make it so. What He found in our world was hate and jealousy and misunderstanding and betrayal and sorrow and — a Cross. Did He surrender to these things? Never. He made them surrender to Him. Did he merely submit to them? Not at all. He seized them and turned them to profit. And when life treated Him to its utmost villainy, spitting in His face and nailing Him to a

Cross, He took hold of that Cross and fashioned it into a
ladder of love and light up which He climbed to His throne
of leadership and lordship in the hearts of earth's millions.

Yes, life belonged to Him, and when we belong to Him,
then life belongs to us. I hear Him talking to His disciples
one day. No rosy road is this which He is showing them:
"They shall lay their hands on you," says He, "delivering
you up to the synagogues and into prisons, being brought
before kings and rulers for my name's sake." But He did
not stop there: "And it shall turn to you for a testimony."
There you have it: the Christian triumphancy of life! Your
obstacles will be your opportunities, says this Master of
our lives. Men may revile you: it will be an occasion for
God's love to be revealed through you. The reviling will be
turned to a revelation. Hardships may hurl themselves at
you: you will find them opening into a braver, stronger,
more fruitful character. Your difficulties will be turned into
doors! Life belongs to you!

Did it work out? It did. They took Stephen and stoned
him. But he turned it to a testimony: "They saw his face
as it had been the face of an angel." They smote him with
the rocks of their murderous hatred; he smote them with the
radiance of his Christian love. And in that awful moment,
Saul of Tarsus was compelled to say to himself, That man
has the secret: life belongs to him.

4. And, still thinking of Stephen, we may pass on to
Paul's next word: "death," too, belongs to Christ's man.
Paul did more than proclaim this truth: he proved it. When
the executioner's axe was being prepared for him, he gave
his Christian valedictory to life and his Christian salutatory
to death and beyond: "I am now ready to be offered and the
time of my departure is at hand. I have fought a good fight,
I have finished my course, I have kept the faith. Henceforth
there is laid up for me a crown of righteousness which the
Lord, the righteous judge, shall give to me at that day, and

141

not to me only but unto all them also which love his appearing." Death belonged to Paul.

After Paul came a noble company of men whom we call the Church Fathers. One of them was the eloquent and courageous Chrysostom. When the Roman emperor threatened him with banishment if he continued to be a Christian, Chrysostom replied, "You cannot banish me, for the world is my Father's house, and you cannot banish me from that." "I will take away your treasure," said the emperor. "That," said Chrysostom, "is impossible, for my treasure is in heaven." "But I will drive you from men, and you will not have a friend left." "Nay, you cannot, for I have a Friend in heaven from whom you cannot possibly separate me." "I will slay you," said the emperor. "That," answered Chrysostom, "you cannot do, for my life is hid with Christ in God." Death belonged to him! How? Because he belonged to One who had mastered death and left behind an empty tomb.

5. Paul takes one more look around at the possessions of the Christian soul. Then he adds, "things present or things to come!" Here is a brace of assets that belong to such a soul. Are you Christ's? Then the present is yours, as capital for investment; and the future also is yours, as the sure day when you shall realize the dividends on what you have invested.

Make the present yours, in Christ's name and for Christ's sake, and then have no anxieties about the future. Some people are always promising themselves and the world that tomorrow they will make the high decision, tomorrow they will tackle the urgent problem, tomorrow they will break the wretched habit, tomorrow they will dedicate themselves to better things. All the while God is saying, in tones now gentle, now thunderous, "Behold, now is the accepted time. Behold, today is the day of salvation."

So put your hand in His now, I beg you, and then rest assured that you shall have His good companionship along every road of life up which your feet, whether eager or aching, may ever take you. Then you may say, in death as in life:

>"No matter what my birth may be,
> No matter where my lot is cast,
>I am the heir in equity
> Of all the precious past.
>
>The art, the science and the lore,
> Of all the ages long since dust,
>The wisdom of the world in store,
> Are mine, all mine in trust.
>
>The beauty of the living earth,
> The power of the golden sun,
>The present, whatso'er my birth,
> I share with every one.
>
>As much as any man am I
> The owner of the working day;
>Mine are the minutes as they fly
> To save or throw away.
>
>And mine the Future to bequeath
> Unto the generations new;
>I help to shape it with my breath,
> Mine as I think or do.
>
>Present and Past my heritage,
> The Future laid in my control;—
>No matter what my name or age,
> I am a Christian soul."

XIV.

What Can You Say to Death?

Text: "*O death, where is thy sting? O grave, where is thy victory?*"—I CORINTHIANS 15:55.

WHEN the monster of war stalks the earth, death is always at his rear, and only a step or two behind. During hostilities the war offices of all the belligerent nations had to work overtime on their relentlessly lengthening casualty lists. Notwithstanding the amazing skill with which the medical men salvaged the wounded, the terse phrase, "killed in action," made its way with a trampling sort of cruelty into scores of thousands of our homes.

In addition to the men in uniform whose lives have been taken as a part of war's bitter cost, there are the vastly larger numbers who die because of the appalling dislocations and distresses which always accompany any large-scale international conflict. Dr. Hambro, late president of the League of Nations, was responsible for the statement that because of World War I not less than thirty-five million human beings died of starvation and epidemics. One shudders to think of the toll of starvation which Europe and the Orient are having to pay in consequence of the war.

To be sure, there is a sense in which war does not give us an extra amount of dying. It is a part of our human lot to be marked for death. That lad of twenty who failed to "come through" at St. Lo or the Ardennes or on Leyte, might have

144

lived to be eighty, but he could not expect to put off death much beyond that point. What we face in such days as these is a dramatic heightening of the fact of death. Death is concentrated in age-groups and in strange places and in ugly ways, to which we are unaccustomed. Death takes the headlines. Death thrusts itself into our consciousness in new and peculiarly poignant ways. Many of us face it as a *fact* — death has recently invaded our circle of love. Many more of us face it as a *fear* — it is an unpleasant possibility that hangs tremulously over some dear one of ours or, indeed, over ourselves.

The question I raise in this message is: Do we have what it takes to face up to death? Do you? Do I? Can we meet it head-on with the confidence that we are not death's victims but death's victors?

Years ago, in my reading, I came across a sentence that etched itself permanently in my memory. In fact the recollection of it is responsible for the wording of today's topic. The sentence was this: "To say something *about* death is easy; to say something *to* death is the test of a valorous faith." Take that sentence and lay it down beside St. Paul's shout of victory in our text: "O death" — the apostle meets death level-eyed — "O death, where is thy sting? O grave, where is thy victory? . . . Thanks be unto God which giveth us the victory through our Lord Jesus Christ."

Not all men can say a thing so triumphant as that in the very teeth of death. Many of them find that the best they can do is to say something *about* it. They somehow lack the assurance that enables them to say something *to* it.

I.

Consider, then, some of the ways in which, indirectly and inadequately, men talk *about* death. One finds that there are two extremes to which they have a tendency to go.

145

Going to one extreme, they say, "Death is nothing." Some-times they say it in a religious and philosophical way. They tell us that mortality, like sin, is only a trick that our morbid imagination plays upon us. They would have us believe that death, along with evil, is unreal, just a fiction of the mind rather than a fact in the universe. It is a mischievous notion that can be cast out by the convenient device of saying to yourself, "Come now, don't be stupid; death has no exis-tence; nobody dies." And so, with a kind of self-hypnosis, and under the guise of philosophy and religion, some of our fellow beings undertake to handle death.

More often, however, the practice of saying that "Death is nothing" takes what might be called a poetic turn. It is customary to grant to poets what is termed "poetic license," and so long as we bear in mind that they *are* taking liberties with facts, little, if any, harm comes from it. On the other hand, it is neither good nor wise to take at face value all that the poets and the poetic interpreters of human experience have had to say about the business of dying. There is Walt Whitman, for example, trying to make out that death is "beautiful." I deny it. The Holy Scriptures deny it. Life itself denies it. I have seen some Christians leave this mortal existence beautifully — this I gladly grant. But that does not mean that the physical fact of death, with all of its associ-ations and consequences, was beautiful. Never!

Arthur Wentworth Hewitt, in his book *Jerusalem the Golden,* offers a fresh study of the Christian view of the future life. In it he has a section on what he calls the "Hor-ror of Death." It contains words of sober wisdom and realism that are long overdue. He is thoroughly in earnest and, I would add, soundly Biblical, when he cries: "I tell you we shall inspire no faith in immortal life by any words which are not faithful to recognize the stark horror of death." He is right.

Recently, while spending a few days in Pasadena, California, I made my way to Mountain View Cemetery. It was a golden morning under a cloudless southern California sky. The cemetery is laid out on a gentle slope at the foot of the Sierra Madre mountains. It contains four graves around which memory and affection twine for me: that of my maternal grandmother Stromberg, whose saintly life was lived before my very eyes in our home when I was a growing boy; that of my youngest brother, who was torn from his violin at seventeen; that of my second-born child, Paul Jr.; and that of my father, who entered the Glory in 1933.

The cemetery itself was beautiful — beautiful, at least, as cemeteries go. But do you mean to tell me that what happened, and is still happening, to the once living, vibrant forms of my dear ones is an empty fiction or a lovely fancy? What of those eyes that once sparkled with good humor or glowed with gentle understanding? What of those hands that once moved with grace and deftness, that once toiled with achieving skill? What of those lips that once felt and responded to love's pressure? Well, it isn't the thing we usually say, for to say it somehow uncovers the stark horror of this desecration we call death; but let us say it, for this once at least. The stubborn, literal truth is that, despite all the loveliness of trees and flowers and grass with which we surround the tombs of our dead, those eyes and hands and lips are slowly rotting in the darkness. And *that,* I tell you, is neither fanciful nor beautiful. The Holy Word of God and the deep instincts of the human heart alike proclaim that death is a reality of ghastly color. It is loathsome. It is a violation. It is hostile. They are therefore wrong who make too little of it.

The other extreme to which men go in talking about death is that of making too much of it. If there are those who shrug their shoulders and say, "Death is nothing," there are others who look out grimly upon the universe and say,

"Death is everything." Death, they say, is the absolute end of the trail for all of us. Death is the end of all things. According to this view it is useless to look for any victory of immortality over mortality, of eternity over time, of hope over despair. Bertrand Russell speaks for this company when he declares that "no fire, no heroism, no intensity of thought and feeling can preserve one individual life beyond the grave."

A few of the poets, too, have joined this fraternity of the faithless. One writes:

> "The world rolls round forever like a mill,
> It grinds out life and death, and good and ill,
> It has no purpose, heart, or mind, or will.

> —————

> "Nay doth it use man harshly, as he saith?
> It grinds him some slow years of bitter breath,
> Then grinds him back into eternal death."

Or this from another poet of despair:

> "From too much love of living,
>   From hope and fear set free,
> We thank with brief thanksgiving
>   Whatever gods may be
> That no life lives forever;
> That dead men rise up never;
> That even the weariest river
>   Winds somewhere safe to sea."

Death, for such persons, becomes, you see, the all-enveloping, all-consuming finality. It takes you back to the philosophy of the worldly pessimist who cries out in the language of Ecclesiastes, "Vanity of vanities, all is vanity and vexation of spirit."

Now let us try to be honest with ourselves: Is it not true that both of these strategies for handling death leave us dissatisfied? To talk about it as though it were a mere trifle or an altogether pleasant dream is simply not being realistic.

It is a form of "kidding" ourselves. On the contrary, to speak *about* it as though it were the hopeless "Dead End" street down which all life is moving, this certainly gives the lie to all our finest hopes and longings, all our highest experiences and capacities. Besides, it doesn't fit us for facing death eye-to-eye and saying something *to* it. Must we be forever content to talk *about* it? Is there no rock of faith upon which we may stand and shout some clear defiance straight at this tireless destroyer who wears a black hood and tramps ceaselessly through our land? Thank God, there is. Let us turn to look at it for a moment.

II.

To put it bluntly, Jesus Christ offers men a faith that enables them to acknowledge the reality of death and at the same time to insist upon the finality and victory of life — life in and through Himself. It is that faith that expresses itself so triumphantly and invincibly in the leaping words of our text: "O death, where is thy sting? O grave, where is thy victory?"

Paul, in this tremendous Resurrection chapter from which we are quoting, takes three views of death: (1) death as we see it in the experience of Jesus, (2) death as we face it in our own human experience, and (3) death as finally overcome and swept away through the resurrection of the body.

Take the death of Jesus and look at it with me, says Paul. As you look at it, remember that it somehow stands related to the whole frightful business of human sin. Then remember that sin is "the sting of death." If there had been no sin, there would have been no death. Death is part of that tragic disaster that has befallen God's world through man's pride and rebellion. If the vicious circle of sin can be broken, if salvation to a new life of harmony with God is possible, then death will have a mortal blow struck at it.

Now lift your eyes to this Jesus on the Cross. He claims to be man's Saviour. He claims to be God in human form, with God's lonely right to forgive sins. He says that He will verify His claims by laying down His life and — here is the staggering thing — by taking it again. What about it? Did He make good or did He not? If His death was the end, then, says Paul, quite openly, we have no Saviour. "If Christ be not raised, your faith is vain; ye are yet in your sins" (v. 17).

But Paul is sure that death was not the end for Jesus. He is sure because, with that keen mind of his, he has examined the evidence of the witnesses. He is convinced that the evidence is clear and overwhelmingly sufficient to satisfy every honest soul. Hence he boldly declares, "But now is Christ risen from the dead, and become the firstfruits of them that slept" (v. 20).

Then Christ *is* the Saviour He claims to be. Then sin *has* met its Conqueror. In humble, sin-confessing penitence you and I can say, "My soul is free: for me, Jesus broke its fetters. My soul is pardoned and washed: for me, Jesus Christ shed His blood. My soul is no longer estranged from God but is in tune with God: for me, Jesus Christ made peace, and now my reconciled heart sings out the joy of oneness with the God of light and love."

If you can say that, cries Paul, then for you death has lost its sting. For you death wears a new aspect. For you it is true that "neither death nor life, nor angels, nor principalities, nor powers, nor things present, nor things to come, nor height, nor depth, nor any other creature shall be able to separate us from the love of God which is in Christ Jesus our Lord." Thus you can say, "O death, where is thy sting? O grave, where is thy victory?"

— This leads naturally to the second view of death that Paul takes as a Christian. He looks at it as the personal experience that must come, soon or late, to each of us, save only those believers who will be alive when Christ returns. To describe the believer's own death, Paul reaches into the vocabulary of the Holy Spirit and brings out a word for death that he got from Jesus. He gives us the word "sleep." Four times over, in varied form, he uses this term to describe the event that brings our Christian pilgrimage to its earthly close. Some of our brethren, says he, are "fallen asleep" (v. 67). "Fallen asleep in Christ" is the phrase he employs in verse 18, while in verse 51 he assures us that we "shall not all sleep."

It should not be difficult for us to understand the meaning of this simple figure of speech. Sleep, as we know it here, is the body's rest, refreshing, and renewal. Very well, "asleep in Christ" means rest for the soul that is made to pass through the experience of death. Rest from pain and weakness! Rest from noise and strife! Rest from care and uncertainty! Rest from storm and strain!

Richard Baxter of Kidderminster was one of the hardest working ministers ever to serve the Church of Christ. He preached with tremendous earnestness. He wrote with untiring zeal. He served his parish with unceasing care and affection. His last hours were spent in great pain, so much so that he once said to his friends, "Do not think the worse of religion for what you see me suffer." To a visitor who called on him the day before he died he said, "I have pain, there is no arguing against sense; but I have peace." When a little later, the friend asked him how he was, he whispered, serenely and radiantly, *"Almost well!"* With that he fell asleep in Christ. And this again is but another way of saying, It is the answer, full and glorious, to the believer's prayer: "O death, where is thy sting? O grave, where is thy victory?"

> *"I pray Thee, Saviour, keep*
> *Me in Thy love,*
> *Until death's holy sleep*
> *Shall me remove*
> *To that fair realm where, sin and sorrow o'er,*
> *Thou and Thine own are one for evermore."*

151

There is one more look at death which the apostle takes as he completes the context of this triumphant shout, "O death, where is thy sting?" He looks forward to the day of consummation that is surely to come — the day when, as he expresses it, "the trumpet shall sound" and Christ shall manifest Himself once more in utter magnificence and in rapturous glory. Listen to Paul as he describes it: "Behold, I shew you a mystery; we shall not all sleep, but we shall all be changed, in a moment, in the twinkling of an eye, at the last trump: for the trumpet shall sound, and the dead shall be raised incorruptible, and we shall all be changed" (vs. 51, 52). That is, there will be a resurrection of the dead, and the risen body, unlike the one that was buried, will be incorruptible. At the same time there will be a transfiguration of the living believers and the transfigured body, unlike the mortal body, will be immortal. The shout of the risen ones will be, "O death, where is thy sting?" The shout of the transfigured ones, who will never taste death, will be, "O grave, where is thy victory?" and the grand and unending shout of all together will be, "Thanks be to God, which giveth us the victory through our Lord Jesus Christ."

It is then, in that grand finale, that there shall be brought to pass the saying, "Death is swallowed up in victory." Of course, you can ask questions that are not easy to answer. You can ask, for example, *how* am I to recognize my dear ones, they in their glorified forms and I in mine? As for myself, I am content with the notion that love's intuitions, which are so astonishing here, will be even more acute over there.

Of course, you can ask, Will my little fellow who died at three have the size and features that are so vividly fixed in my memory? To which, I think, the true answer may be found in this very chapter we are studying. "It is sown," says the Holy Spirit, "a natural body; it is raised a spiritual body." The body is the organ of the soul — that is its function. And bodies are as individually distinct as souls. The connection between the body that is buried and the one that will be raised does not consist of an absolute identity of particles, but of an identity of function, with each resurrected body becoming a perfect expression of the spirit.

You see all of our talk about the appearance of the body at this age or that, under this condition or that, is concerned, often unconsciously, with the ever-dying physical organism that is ours now. The skin is firm at seven and wrinkled at seventy. But death was already working in the body even at seven. It was a small body at two and large at twenty, but for all that it was a dying body.

The one immense, immeasurable, sublime fact about our resurrection body will be its *deathlessness*. Whatever its form, it will be perfectly adapted to our soul. Its form, however, is not so important as the fact that from it will have been removed all of the effects of death, direct and indirect, forever and ever. In all that fair society of the redeemed not one maimed or mutilated body! Not one sightless eye! Not one unhearing ear! Not one withered or missing arm! Not one feeble step! Not one hacking cough! Not one twinge of pain! Not one expiring breath! Not one lifeless form!

The victory will be complete. Christ will be crowned the everlasting Conqueror. God will be all in all. Death, like some haunting, hideous nightmare, will be swept away — utterly and eternally.

"O death, where is thy sting? O grave, where is thy victory?"

You can say *that* to death — if you have Christ!